MW00344446

RIDING THROUGH IT

Equestrian Women Tested & Tranformed

Written by Nikki Porter
&
16 Equestrian Coauthors:
Amber Holm, Antonia Feldkamp, Caroline Archibald,
Betsy Vonda, Brianna Graham, Danielle Crowell, Danielle
Small, Kathleen Arrowsmith, Lexi Busse, Mindy Schneider,
Montana Madill-Laye, Nadine Smith, Stefanie Ly, Teresa
Alexander-Arab, Teresa LaFrance, & Tracey Gibbons

———

EQUI *Muse*
PRESS

Riding Through It: Equestrian Women Tested & Transformed Copyright 2021 by Nikki Porter.

All rights reserved. No part of this publication may be reproduced, distributed or transmitted in any form or by any manner whatsoever, including scanning, photocopying, recording, or other electronic or mechanical methods, without the prior written permission of the publisher, except in the case of brief quotations embodied in critical reviews.

This book is written for entertainment purposes only. It is not intended for personal or equestrian advice. Choosing actions based on the reading of this book will be based on the reader's own judgement after personal reflection and consulting with trusted professionals in the area of their need. The views express herein are not necessarily those of the publisher, nor co-authors.

For permission requests, email Nikki Porter Coaching at:
nikki@nikkiporter.ca

Published by EquiMuse Press
www.nikkiporter.ca

Book design by Offshoot Creative Consulting

To order additional copies of this book write:
nikki@nikkiporter.ca

This book is dedicated to every equestrian who has been tested and transformed by their love of horses and who continues to strive to improve the life of their horse through knowing and understanding themselves.

TABLE OF CONTENTS

INTRODUCTION

BY NIKKI PORTER

———

HORSES HAVE THE potential to inspire and impact every area of an equestrian's life. When we enact our love of horses through riding, ownership, education, business, and competition, it is safe to say that equestrians would not be who or where they are today without their connection to horses. Being an equestrian has the potential to shape how they work, how they communicate, how they parent, and their future vision of themselves.

I say this without hesitation because not only have I directly experienced this incredible impact, having committed to living as an equestrian, so has each equestrian author sharing their story on these pages.

We describe ourselves as "horse people" and sometimes we describe ourselves as crazy too. Perhaps that goes hand in hand with deciding to love something so deeply. That love has the potential to make or break us—depending on how open we are to learning the lessons horses teach us. We are proud to be among the world's horse people, and the stories we share with you on these pages will show you why, strengthen your pride as a horse person, or maybe even make you wish you were one too.

When we began putting together the criteria for this book, it was never intended for it to be restricted to equestrian women. That happened organically and magically. We had interest from both men and women, but when it came time to commit to sharing their story with the world, these equestrian women showed up with open hearts, ready to make an impact on those who are called to read their words.

When we met as a group for the first time on Zoom at the beginning of this project, I could clearly see why each of us were called to and brought together in this way. As each woman introduced themselves to the rest of the authors, the feelings of connection, understanding, compassion, and support was tangible.

Our first-time meeting as a group of equestrian authors, vulnerably and ready to share our stories with the world, proved to Nadine and me that this project was going to be exactly what we had hoped for. It was an opportunity to offer equestrians a space to write, share, connect, and celebrate with like-minded horse people in a supportive environment. It felt like we hit the equestrian-author jackpot with the women you'll meet in this book. Their stories meld their energy, love, experience, lessons, and desire to come together. It all felt so right.

In this book, you will read stories of loss, heartbreak, grief, fear, pain, and rock bottom, but because of horses, you will also see them transform into stories of resilience, love, awareness, self-acceptance, confidence, compassion, and awakenings. No two stories are alike. Each writer and the experiences they share with us are as unique as they are, but there is a thread that weaves each story together and connects every equestrian in the world: Horses test and transform us.

With love,

Nikki
Owner, Founder
Nikki Porter Coaching & (co)Informed Equestrian

CHAPTER 1

GRACE AND GRIT

BY CAROLINE ARCHIBALD

———

I HAVE NEVER BEEN the horse girl so many young ladies are, so my
introduction and experiences are unique. I would go so far as to say the
original Quarter Horse power was a vital part of my midlife "awakening."
I could never have imagined such a gift as horses, one which came to us but
was never intended for myself, to bring me to where I am today as a woman
and a horsewoman.

My youngest son has always been interested in farms and agriculture.
With my eldest son on a youth exchange in Belgium, I was able to dedicate my
time and attention to Jack exclusively. I inquired about riding lessons, and so
many people spoke highly of Sweet's Horse Center. Upon reaching out to the
owner, a first lesson was quickly arranged for Jack. When I went to share the
news with my husband and son, Jack was thrilled, and Trevor quickly went
on the record as saying, "We are not buying a horse!" *No dear, we are not buying
a horse.*

The day arrived for Jack's lesson. His instructor was a lovely lady named
Janie. Jack was introduced to his new adventure; we both had no idea at that
moment we would meet a four-legged buckskin also named Jack. Jack-the-
boy was in absolute awe. Buckskins were his favorite, and my heart felt an

1

immediate connection to the people and horses involved because my paternal great grandparents were Janie and Jack. It all felt right.

As the weeks progressed, Jack-the-boy wanted to spend more time with Jack-the-horse. I have always been in favor of giving experiences rather than material things, so with the Christmas holidays approaching, I inquired about leasing Jack-the-horse. Discussing this with my husband, I was quickly reminded, "We are not buying a horse!" *No dear, we are not buying a horse.*

We had a very happy teenage boy who opened his gift Christmas morning to see a lease for Jack. His joy added something positive to an otherwise lonely Christmas for us, whereby we were missing Andrew, our other son who was in Belgium. I love the magic of the season and the celebration of a miracle, and this certainly felt like a miracle and will remain one of my favorite memories.

Jack soon discovered the horse center also had a dairy farm, so time with the horses was soon conflicted. We experienced our first shift at this time with Jack so interested in seeing the cows and helping with the milking that I became the care person for Jack-the-horse. I had no idea grooming him and building trust would bring back so many memories from my childhood I thought I had dealt with but learned it was through avoidance and burying.

Jack-the-horse had experienced physical trauma during his previous training that resulted in damage to his poll area, which I quickly learned from my training in the dental world is equivalent to the debilitating TMJ disorder. I approached Jack in a totally different way than he had ever experienced by respecting his past and personal space. A gentle touch began to build trust and confidence and release some of the pressure he was carrying as a protection mechanism.

Within no time, Jack-the-horse went from a horse who really did not care to be brought in from the herd, to a horse that lifted his head and eventually started to walk toward me when he saw me. He also went from a horse that bolted to return to the safety of the herd when released back in the pasture, to a horse that allowed removal of his halter and happily accepted a peppermint, which was my Great-Grandpa Jack's special treat. Jack-the-horse let us know pink peppermints were the ultimate.

An issue arose when I was spending time with Jack-the-horse, and Jack-the-boy would appear for his lessons. Suddenly, Jack-the-horse did not want to engage with Jack-the-boy. This put me in an awkward position because I never intended to create such a strong bond with my son's horse. It got to the point where I could not be in the stable when Jack had a lesson. I did not want either of my boys upset with me. Other boarders commented on the changes in Jack-the-horse and how much personality he had hidden inside. Once he felt comfortable and secure, the true Jack shone through.

By this time, spring had arrived. My family and I went South for a holiday during March break. Mid-week, I received a message from the barn owner informing me that she was following her passion and selling all her horses. Because we leased Jack, we would have the first opportunity to purchase him. I felt my stomach sink as my husband's words 'We are not buying a horse,' played in my head. I did not want to upset Jack and ruin a holiday, so I kept the news to myself until we were home.

Reality came crashing down following vacation with this new element added to our return home. I recalled my conversation with the owner and that regardless of the timeline, I could not see ownership happening. Of course, Jack-the-boy was disappointed and upset. My husband Trevor quickly reminded us of his concern from day one. I cannot explain the gut-wrenching feeling I experienced the moment when I knew I needed to purchase this horse.

Upon a much-heated discussion, I decided *we* weren't buying a horse; *I* was. I initially felt guilty because I had never spent such an amount of money without my husband's support, but my intuition remained strong. I needed this horse, and perhaps he needed me. By this time, Jack was spending less time at the horse barn and every free minute at the dairy barn and soon had a job at a local dairy farm.

I knew enough that Jack-the-horse had a value, and if I could not manage to make this work, I could sell him and recoup most of my investment. I was confident this would not have to happen; when I commit, I do not waver, but it helped to know, nonetheless.

I left the barn many nights in tears of frustration, needing to get the tears out before I stepped into my home because I knew I would not be able to get support in anything related to the horse. It was a subject avoided at all costs.

My heart was stubborn enough not to give up, and over time, with patience and trust, the tears became less frequent. I knew I needed to learn

3

so much and felt at a disadvantage because I was older; I was still learning how to be a horse girl. I reached out to one of the instructors at the barn I felt most comfortable with. Much to my delight, she agreed to take me on and she proved to have the patience of a saint.

It felt very much like I was in a trial by fire at times, but there were more good days than bad, and with a new relationship being established with the goal of a partnership, we were quickly establishing our roles.

Consistency was important and Jack would learn what was expected of him. The greatest lesson I learned through this process was to be clear in my communication. If I was not clear, Jack would become frustrated, and things would spiral quickly. I soon became aware of what was happening between us and was amazed at how magical nights were when we connected.

Never could I have imagined the parallels I would share with a horse. I know I connected with Jack-the-horse so profoundly because I, too, had experienced trauma as a result of the unanticipated actions of someone I trusted. Growing up, I witnessed an unhappy marriage between my parents and a shift in family dynamics. I experienced mental and physical abuse at the hands of someone who was supposed to be there to protect me.

To survive, I quickly learned to shut myself off and not trust people, especially those claiming to love me. I have always had a fighting spirit and was able to take every bit of courage I had to confide to my paternal grandparents and thereafter, have safety and security around me.

I have read and heard it said by mentors that a horse is a mirror reflection of ourselves and my personal experience has found this to be true. Jack's energy is quickly elevated when he feels threatened, and I believe this to be true of any prey animal. Regardless of what humans do, horses will always be prey animals. The magic that they even allow us the pleasure and experience of climbing on their backs and riding is beyond my comprehension, and I believe they should be held sacred.

I have learned to be aware of my own energy and know it also runs high, which I believe was ingrained in me as a protective mechanism. Jack has taught me to be aware of this, and when I keep this in check, and he feels this shift, he knows I am trustworthy, and he is able to show his true self. Jack needs clear communication and expectations, much like myself. I have always been amazed at his patience with me.

Early on in our journey, I was incredibly afraid I'd ruin him. I had no idea how much of a perfectionist I was until I started riding lessons at the age of forty-two with no prior experience, other than the tourist traps on various holidays I have been privileged to take. Riding was a very humbling experience. I am not athletic by any means, and sports were not an option during my childhood.

We spent a tremendous amount of time on groundwork, which allowed me to get a feel and build trust. I appreciate my instructor's words of encouragement that everything done on the ground could be done in the saddle. This process also taught me to slow my pace and energy down. I had no idea this was the case because I didn't know what I didn't know. Unwittingly, at first I put a great deal of pressure on Jack with my high energy and abruptness. My mind for so long had been *go, go, go*, and I found to slow things down was a real challenge for me.

The amazing gift that I have learned from horses is that the past doesn't matter, and the future means nothing to them. The important focus is the present—what a gift to enjoy the right here, in the right now. I needed right here, right now.

I was ashamed of my past and so afraid of the future that was created with my husband and sons. It was as if I didn't trust it to last, so I kept a distance so as not to get attached. On some level I believed that if I did this, I wouldn't miss it when it was gone.

Touch has always been something that I have struggled with because of my childhood trauma. Apart from my sons, I was very uncomfortable with touch and, as a result, closed myself off and blocked people from getting too close, physically and emotionally. Anything I allowed to get close to me had the potential to leave me, so I quickly learned it was far easier for me if I remained unattached.

Jack was described to me as a "sensitive" horse which always struck me as interesting. I find it fascinating how we put labels on our horses and ourselves—labels that may or may not be accurate. Thinking about my own labels, I am often considered standoffish and closed. Our labels become a way for the world around us to make sense of us, and when we allow them to define our horse and ourselves, the wrong story is often told.

With Jack's trauma and negative experience with strong physical pressure, I became very mindful of the relationship I wanted to have with him. I wanted it based on respect and softness, rather than fear-based and physical. An early liberty clinic we participated in at our barn created the blueprint for the partnership I wanted with Jack. The clinician described being so in sync with your horse that if there was ever a burning building, your horse would not bolt but would walk beside you, trusting your leadership.

This understanding was so powerful to me in so many ways. It made me aware of the herd dynamic and how vital it was that Jack felt safe with me and how I had an obligation to him to be the best horsewoman I could be. Part of this was the necessity to build my human herd to support my goals of riding my horse and having us both enjoy the experience and look forward to being together again.

Jack has a physical scar across his nose—constant reminder of the physical pain he experienced along the way—that always made me feel sad for him. My revamped desire for our partnership transformed into a reminder not to get caught in the trap of perfectionism. So many things will be damaged in the constant pursuit of perfection which in reality does not exist.

Life is constantly changing and being able to adapt and pivot—to be resilient—is key. I don't think this became any more obvious than with the global pandemic beginning in March of 2020. It is a period that I am certain will remain in our memories for a very long time. I know it is a year I will recall as bittersweet.

My dad's health had been declining the past number of years. As I mentioned in the beginning, when I was nine, my parents, like many of my generation, divorced. My dad was a long-distance truck driver and had met the love of his life on the road, an American woman. This resulted in a complex relationship between me and my dad. I am thankful we always had a connection that I truly believe time or distance could not erase. Lifestyle and extreme drive and determination led to several health issues for my dad.

The call I had been dreading for many years finally came that Dad was in the hospital four hours away from where I lived. Dad spent over a month in the hospital, and I made a trip every other day to spend the day with him and drove home once he was fed and settled for the night. My first stop before arriving home to my family was to the barn to see Jack. Regardless of the hour of day or darkness, Jack would be there and allow me to sit quietly with him and breathe in his warm earthy scent and just be.

Dad ended up moving in with my family. On a good day, I would load him up, oxygen tank and all, and take him out to the barn for a Jack visit. He always had a peppermint which Jack would gladly accept from the passenger seat of my car. I would do some groundwork in the parking lot, and Dad would give his feedback. I was pleasantly surprised and entertained as he would tell stories of horses his grandparents had on the farm when he was a child.

As Dad became weaker and his health declined, trips to the pasture became too much for him. I had to prioritize my time which meant a dramatic reduction in the time I spent with Jack. I also decided at this time to step away from our dental clinic because Dad's care was too demanding and I could not be in both places.

COVID-19 certainly made it difficult to have help come in, but I know my dad would never have allowed that anyway. He was a very private, proud man and so very stubborn. I know I have this streak in me, too, and I also see it in my son Jack. One thing I'm determined to do is channel my stubbornness in a positive way. I do not want to become jaded and isolated; I want to be open and real.

Jack-the-horse has made me aware of my limitations and has taught me to be patient and clear in my intentions. My observation is that the more rigid and closed off a person is, the more softness is required.

This created one of the largest shifts in my life so far. My dad was full of regret for his life choices and for abandoning me as a child. I certainly was once resentful of the time I missed with my dad, but I forgave him long ago and got to enjoy the relationship he had with my boys.

I have never seen my dad in tears, and I am doubtful he had seen me in tears since I was a little girl. To be able to offer forgiveness, compassion, and safety was greater than any gift I could have given him, and it felt like a great weight off me to be open and authentic while his care was palliative.

I was able to provide a safe and loving space for him, and we spent his final days together. I learned so much about him during that time, and I learned so much about myself in the process. I knew I was strong because I have had no other choice in my life but to be, but my experience with Jack also taught me to be soft, and softness takes much more strength than weakness and facilitates a powerful connection with ourselves and others.

Dad passed away the day before Christmas Eve. With the pandemic, my oldest son who then lived in P.E.I. could not come home for the holidays. My husband also lost his grandmother two days before Dad's passing. We were experiencing so much loss and pain at an emotional time, and COVID-19 added a whole new element of isolation, which seemed cruel.

Jack brought me the greatest comfort because there were no words or expectations. We could both just be. I felt so incredibly guilty for not spending the time with him we both had grown accustomed to. I found he was initially not as interested in being with me after my hiatus. Trust had to be re-established and was on Jack's terms.

The loss of my time in the dental clinic was a significant shift and adjustment for me. It was something I had built with my husband over twenty years ago and it quickly moved forward without me. The excess amount of time I then had, without anything to fill it, was difficult for me. My brain had a hard time accepting the stillness. Having a purpose of going to the barn to care for Jack kept me moving forward rather than spiraling into a dark place. My husband, who never wanted a horse, finally saw the transformative power this horse had on me and admitted he was happy I had the horse.

Jack had put on weight while not being worked or ridden over that past year and a half. I felt guilty for his condition and it was hard to laugh off the observations of fellow boarders: "Jack is *so* round." *Yes, yes, he was.* When I started riding him again, it became apparent something was off. My gut told me it was more than my inexperience. I reached out to my tribe, and Jack received a massage and magnetic therapy, which certainly did not hurt Jack, but we could not seem to get clean movement.

A fellow boarder was having a young vet come to treat her horse with chiropractic treatments, and she invited me to have Jack join the time slot if I was interested. I jumped at the opportunity, but I was going to have a conflict as it was Jack-the-boy's high school graduation.

Luckily, multitasking is what we women do best. Jack was able to go first, and the vet immediately noticed lameness issues. I felt a great sense of relief and hope, knowing we were finally on a path to finding answers.

Flexion tests were done, and nerve-block injections were given to locate the issue in Jack's left leg. I had invited my coach, who had also treated Jack with massage, and a lovely young lady who would also be riding him. I wanted to ensure that Jack's human herd was as solid as his horse herd.

Radiographs were taken while I was at my son's graduation, and upon my return, it was discovered Jack had a broken bone in his knee, and excess bone resulted as his body repaired the dislocation. Images were sent to the veterinary college in P.E.I. for confirmation that the bone could be removed with surgery. Talk about a day of high emotions. I worked my way through it with an extremely grateful heart to have answers and trust in this young vet's knowledge and skills and at the same time, see my son's successful end to an important chapter in all our lives.

Within a few days, we had a confirmed diagnosis and a new challenge. Jack had developed arthritis in his knee from the trauma. Surgical splinting was an option and would not guarantee riding soundness in his future. Plan B was to do an injection in his knee, which would need to be done periodically.

Jack responded to the injections as well as we could hope. He is moving the best he's ever moved since I have owned him. I can't change the past, and nothing positive comes from dwelling on it. When we know better, we do better. Our focus is enjoying the here and now, and our mantra has become "stay with me right here, right now" as we take a deep breath together.

About Caroline Archibald

———

Caroline has been married for twenty-three years to her high school sweetheart. She is Mum/Mama to her two greatest blessings Andrew and Jack.

She is a graduate of St. Francis Xavier University and currently runs a successful dental practice with her husband Trevor, dentist extraordinaire. Caroline expanded the services offered at the clinic by opening a clinical skincare studio, Fleur, during the height of the pandemic, which continues to flourish.

Writing has always been a passion, and Caroline found this project presented itself at a critical time to tell this, her equestrian journey which led to personal growth and healing.

Jack-the-boy is in his first year at Dalhousie Agricultural College in the Dairy Management Program, chasing his dreams.

Dedication

To Trevor, Andrew, and Jack for creating a safe sanctuary and filing my life with so much love. xo

BOOK RECOMMENDATIONS

The Untethered Soul by Michael Singer
Light is the New Black by Rebecca Campbell
The Gifts of Imperfection by Brené Brown
The Conscious Communicator: The Pursuit of Joy and Human Connection Inspired by the Art of Horsemanship by Nikki Porter

CHAPTER 2

SHE BRIGHTENED

BY LEXI BUSSE

———

TO THIS DAY, I feel like I played a massive trick on my parents, and they still have not caught on. I began my journey with horses nearly twenty years ago when I was eight years old. I, being the typical eight-year-old, went through a phase of horse obsession. Perhaps not so typical was my immense stubbornness and resolve, which led to the gift of three introductory lessons at the closest lesson barn an hour and a half away. Those three lessons evolved into six more lessons, and then six more, and then into a summer riding camp.

Finally, my parents decided to sign me up for Pony Club and the weekly lessons that came with it. My parents should probably be canonized for driving me back and forth every week, and then twice a week, and then three times a week until I turned sixteen. Even then, they still accompanied me to my Pony Club lessons after school so I would not be too tired from the drive. It was a lot; the time, the gas, the lessons, the leasing, and then the purchasing of a horse. They did not complain—much.

My parents didn't overly complain because they saw what I gained from it. They saw their shy little girl making real friends for the first time in her life. They saw their daughter, who had already battled mental health issues at the tender age of six, become confident and driven. They saw me learn the true meanings of love, commitment, and grit. They saw my heart ripped open by tragedy and how my horse, and the community of horse people, taught me how to mend it. They saw me fall and cry and bleed and get up again even when I was afraid. Those are the lessons you cannot put a price tag on.

And so, I became an equestrian. I spent my weekends and summers at the barn. I spent every dollar I earned on farrier and vet bills. I tried to read every book and learn every secret about horsemanship and riding. Life happened, I grew up, I went to university, boys came and went, but horses remained.

Through all that time, I can think of nearly a dozen stories where horses have healed me and a few when I healed horses at the same time. Each instance holds meaning and memory. The story that I want to tell is not just a story about me; it is the story of me, and Paige, and the horse that rescued us both.

A few years into my riding career, a girl at our barn had imported a horse from Holland. This was a great novelty in little ol' Saskatoon, and I remember it being a pretty big deal. Rex was fancy and talented and everything you expected from an *import*. I was quite young then, but I knew with utmost certainty that I would never own such a gallant steed as Rex. I did not even think to dream of it. That was a one-off, a special circumstance for a wealthy family, and it was not something I would ever have in my life, or so I thought.

Over time importing a horse from Europe was not quite the inaccessible thing that it once had been. So, over the years, several of my riding peers, Paige included, made the trek over to Europe to buy horses that better fit their needs.

At the time, I was riding a horse that was not suited to me and caused me to seriously question my abilities as an equestrian. Frustrated with the over-priced market in Canada, I told my coach to keep her eye out for a horse for me on her next shopping excursion.

When she came home, she told me she had found a horse that was absolutely perfect and that if I didn't buy him, she would find someone else who would. My parents silently cursed the day I had ever asked for riding lessons, and Remy became mine.

And so, I called Remy my "better than a dream horse."

Remy was a breath of fresh air. My last horse had been a dirty stopper who could, in the same day, could go from winning a class to stopping at the second jump and dropping me on my face. Remy was honest, careful, and patient, even when I asked the wrong questions. Remy brought me into the jumper ring, where I had longed to be for many years, and we found success. I became ten times the rider I was before, and it is all due to him. Is he perfect? No, he has his quirks and idiosyncrasies, and so do I. But he is perfect for me.

Paige and I had started riding at the same time, although she was a few years younger than me and much more naturally talented. To be honest, I was often a little jealous of her. It is hard to be fourteen and struggling with a hyper, naughty Thoroughbred at your very first horse show and watch a ten-year-old flying around courses with ease and placing in every class. It is harder to be fifteen and struggling with that same difficult Thoroughbred in the same 2'6" hunter classes and watch an eleven-year-old sailing around the jumper ring with her beautiful warmblood.

The jealousy never lasted long, though. One of the most important skills you learn as an equestrian is that you will save yourself a lot of time and negativity when you learn to celebrate the success of your friends rather than comparing yourself to them. Over the years Paige went to other provinces and even to California to train and compete. One year she qualified to go to the Royal Winter Fair in Toronto. Throughout her success, she was always humble, hard-working, and devoted to her horses and the art of riding. The horse always came first.

As we grew older, we reached the age where a four-year age gap no longer precluded a close friendship. I would stay over at her house during horse shows, and we would go on spontaneous shopping trips while at shows in other cities. She started working with a personal trainer, and soon I found myself awake at 6 am doing boot camp workouts with her and some other barn friends. We were in the same lesson group and bonded over our successes and trials.

When Paige graduated high school, I was well into my undergraduate degree. It was a bittersweet day at the barn when she checked her email before a lesson and found out that she had been accepted into McGill University. I was thrilled—and, again, a little jealous—that she had been accepted into her dream school. I was also incredibly sad that she was moving across the country. After she left, we drifted apart, as often happens when life changes.

I was ecstatic to see her when she came home for the holidays and thrilled to have her back in the barn during the summer.

I did not know then that the Paige who had left was not quite the same Paige that came back. Shortly before she left for university, she had been diagnosed with a chronic illness that meant she had to stop riding for a while. That, and a combination of intense medications and moving away from everything and everyone she had ever known, sent her down a mental health spiral.

It was a cold and bleak January day when I first learned that Paige had been admitted to the hospital. Nobody I knew was quite sure why she was there, but we assumed for the most part that it had something to do with her chronic illness. The hospital was attached to the university, and my friend from the barn and I decided to visit her during a break in classes. We met at the hospital's Starbucks. The three of us chatted and caught up, and finally, I broached the subject of her hospital stay.

"How long are you going to be here?" I asked.

"I'm not sure, at least a month," she admitted.

"Really? Is it your liver?"

A pause.

"No, um, I'm in the psych ward."

Her words hit me like a punch in the gut. Paige? In the psych ward? Paige? My always-smiling, energetic, Paige?

In retrospect, I was mad at myself for not knowing before that she had been struggling. I felt like I, of all people, should have known, should have seen the signs. I had spent years wrestling with the faceless demon that was mental illness. I had run the gamut of doctors, therapists, and medications and felt that I was nearly an expert on mental health and wellness. I even taught seminars on managing stress at the university learning center. How did I not know that my friend was battling the same demons?

"Oh," was all I could manage to say.

She had been putting on a brave face until then—just a girl meeting her friends for a coffee. Now, the cat was out of the bag, and she cracked a little. Her composure slipped, and she quickly looked away.

When horses spook at something, there are three options for what they might do: Fight, flight, or freeze. Being prey animals, when they are scared, they

15

usually choose to flee. If they are not sure whether something is frightening or not, they tend to freeze first, assess, and then flee. It takes a lot of training and a lot of trust in their rider for them to break out of that state. One thing I had learned when I rode a young, spooky horse was that if you could keep them from freezing and if you could keep their feet moving, their thoughts would stop racing. If you can trot past the scary thing, it becomes a lot less scary. So, I took a breath and kept moving.

"Paige, whatever you need, whatever I can do, I am here." I said, keeping my voice steady.

She brightened.

"Do you want to come and see my room?"

Go into the psych ward? No, no, I did not. I had been working my entire life to stay as far away from that place as possible. As far as I was concerned, all psychiatric wards were the stuff of nightmares and Hollywood movies. Even the name made me shudder. But this was Paige. She was my friend. And she needed her friends. I reminded myself: *Keep your feet moving.*

"Yes, yes, of course! Let's go!" I said with fake enthusiasm.

In truth, it was not that bad. There were neither screaming patients nor nurses with restraints and sedatives hanging from their belts. It was bright, with big windows, and art on the walls. There was good food and genuinely kind counselors. It was a place to get better.

As the visit continued, I realized that it was the place that Paige needed to be. She told me about the events leading up to her admission. She was candid about her state of mind, and I had never seen her so vulnerable.

I threw myself into helping her from that day forward, still mad at myself for not recognizing the signs I knew so well. I decided that I was in a unique position to help her in a way that few others could. I visited her three times a week. We would sit together and color, knit, or chat. We talked about horses, about memories of horse shows, and our friends from the barn.

When she started a new course of treatment, I sat and worked on my schoolwork for hours while she slept off the medicine. I made friends with the other patients, and I held her hand when she was scared. I was not a doctor, but I was a scientist. I researched medications, treatments, and physicians. I shared with her the techniques that helped me and that helped others that

I knew. Supporting her became a top priority for me. I even changed her ringtone on my phone to the emergency alarm so that I would always hear it if she called and needed me.

My mom was worried that pouring so much of my energy into Paige would lead to a mental health crisis of my own and she told me so. I understood her concern, but it was not necessary. In fact, it was the opposite. I knew that Paige needed me at my best, and so I took care of myself better than I had for years. I ate well, was consistent at the gym, and booked myself regular massages. When things got hard, and I needed a break from the world, I went directly to the barn to see Remy.

Now, Remy is not a gentle horse. He is impatient, high energy, and has no regard for personal space. He has an attention span of about fifteen minutes and will get antsy if I take more than that to brush him and tack him up for a ride. Remy is also a very smart and intuitive horse, and on those hard days when I arrived after spending an afternoon at the hospital, he knew what I needed. He would settle, nuzzle me gently, and allow me to press my face into his withers and cry, but he wouldn't let me wallow in the sadness.

After he allowed me my ten minutes of emotion, he would patiently but persistently start his "let's get a move on, Mom!" routine. It was his way of reminding me that there was a time to be sad and overwhelmed and feel everything, but I could not hold on to that darkness for too long. It was time to wipe my tears and come back to the land of the light and ride.

The weeks went by, and I was starting to feel a bit desperate because Paige was not really making any progress. The hardest part about mental illness is there is no magic pill that will make everything better. No matter how much I wanted to do something, anything, to help her, I could not just flip a switch and make the demons retreat. Some days she was on so many medications that I was not sure she even knew I was there. Some days I felt like she had given up, and there was no fight left in her. I felt helpless and scared.

Then came a day when Paige told me she was going to be given a day pass to leave the hospital. Her doctors instructed her to do something that she loved. Tentatively, Paige asked me if she could take a lesson on Remy on that day, and I was thrilled. Finally, I had something I could *do*.

The day before her day pass, I rode Remy to make sure he was on his very best behavior. Paige's chronic illness was still a major concern, and a fall, even a minor one, could cause irreparable damage. I was nervous, but I knew Remy. I knew that this was the most important task I could ask him to perform. I put him through his paces and tuned him up as best as I possibly could. After our ride, I held him close and kissed his nose to share the news with him.

"Listen, buddy," I whispered to him, "I have a really big job for you tomorrow."

Remy sighed and leaned into my face to scratch his forehead against mine.

"I need you to take care of her. I need you to keep her safe. And I need you to remind her what it feels like to fly."

The morning came, and I drove out to the barn super early. It felt like I was getting ready for a show. I curried and brushed Remy until he nearly lost his mind. Paige arrived with coffee for both of us and laughed at my primping and polishing of him.

"You don't have to get him all fancy on my accord, Lex!" She tutted at me as she helped me tack him up.

It was the first time I had seen her outside of the hospital in over a month, and it did my heart good to see her in a more familiar setting and out of the sterile environment that was the hospital ward. We worried for a minute about the IV port that was still in her arm but relied on an old equestrian hack—vet wrap—to keep it protected. We led Remy into the arena, and I whispered once more for him to be good.

Remy was perfect. Paige had not been on the back of a horse in months, but her natural talent shone through, and she looked great on him. He always knew exactly what I needed—when to be still and when to push me. He treated her the same. He did not baby her but carried her with strength and vigor. As they jumped around the arena, I felt a huge wave of relief pass through me.

There was a gleam in her eye that I recognized as Paige, the old Paige, the fierce competitor, and the passionate horsewoman. My heart stopped for a second when she pushed him at a jump. He did not like the distance and refused. She did not fall, thank God, and our coach gave her flack for not setting him up for success. She gritted her teeth and turned him back to it. This time she collected his stride and pushed him into a bouncier pace.

Happier with that ride, he leaped over the jump without a second thought.

I breathed easy again and whispered a thankful prayer for Remy. Not only was he giving her the "something that makes you happy" the doctors had asked for, but he was giving her a normal ride where she had to work a little.

I realized at that moment that in my attempts to help Paige, I had been treating her like a porcelain doll. I was trying to be gentle and positive when I was around her but what she really needed was for me to be normal. I was her access to the world outside of the hospital, and I needed to be real. Remy knew that, and he gave her a feeling of "normal" at a time when everything felt out of her control. She was *living* out in the world instead of merely existing within the walls of the psych ward. That day, as they soared up a bending line, for the first time in a long time I saw my beloved friend truly and freely smile.

I wish I could tell you that an hour's lesson was all it took to cure Paige. That Remy was the magical switch I had been looking for to make it all better. But that's not how life works, and Paige still had a long road in front of her. I can tell you that today, after a lot of work and trials and tribulations, Paige is once again a healthy, happy, and vibrant person.

That day stands out to me as the day I really saw my friend come out from the shadows that were consuming her. The day I began to believe that she really was going to get better, and I would see that smile again soon.

Keep moving your feet.

About Lexi Busse

Lexi grew up in Saskatchewan and has been riding since she was eight years old. She began by taking lessons with Saskatoon Pony Club, where she was an active member until moving to Vancouver in 2020. Pony Club provided her a well-rounded horse education, with a strong emphasis on stable management and horse care. She has shown in hunters and jumpers throughout Western Canada. She is a farm girl at heart and is always most comfortable with a little bit of dirt on her boots.

Outside of the horse world, she studied Anatomy and Cell Biology at the University of Saskatchewan and worked in scientific research for several years.

She is currently a student at the University of Fraser Valley in Abbotsford, British Columbia, and teaches beginner riding lessons at Collingwood Stables in Langley.

Dedication

For Elaine, who molded me into the person I am; for Judy, who never let me give up; and for Paige, thank you for fighting.

Book Recommendations

Daring Greatly by Brené Brown
The Girl Who Loved Wild Horses by Paul Goble

CHAPTER 3

SERENDIPITOUS HEART

BY TRACEY GIBBONS

W E ALL HAVE those times in our lives when things happen out of the blue or line up so perfectly that we think they were heaven-sent—a preordained destiny where everything just falls into place. The right people at the right time or the right horse at the right time. Molly was my right horse at the exact right time. She was the catalyst for so much in my life. I know we were meant to find each other.

I grew up in a very small town in rural Newfoundland, Canada. I was ridiculously shy as a child and spent the first five years of my life attached to my mom's leg. Always, I felt like I was an outsider. I didn't make friends easily and felt awkward and unsure about everything. There was one thing I was one hundred percent sure of: I loved horses. I don't know why I was always so drawn to them, but it was in good part because of their beauty and grace, strength, and companionship, all wrapped up in a gorgeous package.

The community I grew up in was small, so there was no opportunity to take riding lessons or to volunteer at a stable to help out and be around the animals I was drawn to. Over time I put horses into my life in whatever way I could. I drew them; I bought oil paint-by-numbers sets and painted them; I put horse posters all over my walls; I watched every single horse race, show jumping competition, movie, or TV show that had the slightest thing to do with horses.

I dreamed of a day when I would have my very own horse to love, groom, and ride. I envisioned my first horse; she would be my very best friend, my confidant, and my greatest joy. I collected the names of all the horses I watched on TV and wondered when I'd have my own Big Ben, Go For Wand, or Mr. T.

In 1999, I even won the Name the Foal Contest that is held by the breeding program at Spruce Meadows in Calgary, Alberta, Canada, with the name EZ Jumper. I almost lost my mind when I met Ian Millar, Captain Canada himself, and he signed my book. I do believe some tears were shed.

As time passed in my life beyond my horse dreams, I did all the things that I thought I was "supposed" to do. I became a graphic designer, got my first real graphic design job, met a man, fell in love, and ended up leaving Newfoundland behind. Eventually, we moved to my husband's hometown, Woodstock, New Brunswick.

I left everything behind, my family, friends, and an awesome job. I was in a strange province, knowing no one but my family of in-laws. My husband was working non-stop, trying to set up his practice, and I was sitting at home alone. I was miserable.

One auspicious day, while talking to my friend Natalie from back home, she said something that changed the trajectory of my life. After lamenting to her about the state of things, she said, "Tracey, you can never, ever give up on your dreams. What do *you* want to do?"

What did I want to do?

I had gotten so far removed from myself, so wrapped up in doing what was right or what others wanted from me that I had forgotten my own dreams and desires. I took the time and thought about what I wanted, and of course, the answer came in a flash. Horses. I had wanted to be around them my whole life, and that moment seemed the perfect time to pursue that dream.

About a year after moving to Woodstock, I started working at a local car dealership and became friendly with the financial manager, Debbie. She had grown up with a horse and was familiar with the equestrian community in the area. She told me to call Laura Burtt at Green Meadow Stables as she is a certified coach and offered English riding lessons.

Yikes, English riding lessons. What would I hold on to when I lost my balance? I kept telling myself it didn't matter if I sucked at riding. All that mattered was that I was going to be around horses. Finally! I would get to pet them and groom them and *smell* them. This is how you truly know if you've got horse fever—if you love the smell, you're sunk!

Years after wishing and dreaming of a life with horses to any degree, I arrived at my first lesson excited and nervous. I remember getting out of the car and taking a deep breath, relaxing into the smell and the sounds of the barn.

Laura greeted me and brought me to meet one of the lesson horses. Her name was Molly. She was a beautiful little pinto mare. Well-versed in dealing with little kids and novice riders, she didn't give me more than a cursory look; it was all old hat to Molly.

Thanks to my friend Joanne, when Laura asked me if I knew how to groom, I said yes. After watching for a while, Laura deemed me competent enough and left me alone to finish grooming. Molly stood quite still and let me do my thing. She was soft and warm and had such a gentle way about her.

Our first lesson was a slow-motion ride, which was exactly what I needed. At that point, I honestly didn't care if we ever went faster than a slow walk—I was on a horse! I remember thinking I was so high up, which is hilarious now, considering she was only 14.3 hands high. As they say, good things come in small packages. I started riding twice a week, and it was definitely the highlight of my life. The first time I cantered, it took my breath away. It was a feeling of absolute freedom I had never experienced before, a feeling of being one with her and soaring around the arena.

After a year of riding lessons, I decided to lease Molly. This gave me 100% access to her whenever I wanted. I was heading to the barn three to four times a week. The bond between Molly and I was growing all the time. She started nickering to me when she saw me enter the barn. Laura commented that she was a different horse. Apparently, people had called her "Moody Molly" but I didn't know that side of her at all. I knew I wanted her for my own, but as a lesson horse, one that Laura had trained from the age of two, I never thought she would sell her and so, two years after starting riding lessons, I purchased another horse.

His name was Roger. The *Black Beauty* of my dreams, or so I thought. Roger turned out to be a bit of a nightmare. I went from a horse who would ground tie to being pinned up against the stall wall. I had to fight with him to pick out his feet. He would always need to be lunged before being ridden and would pin his ears pretty much the entire time I rode him.

After about six weeks of going to the barn every day and leaving in tears, I finally agreed with Laura when she said she thought he was too much horse for me. I sold him to her, and she put a lot of time and effort into making him a lesson horse at the barn. We found out later on that Roger had quite a few medical conditions, which likely caused pain when he was being ridden. After this discovery, I really didn't blame him for pinning me against the wall, considering he anticipated a ride and, therefore, pain would be forthcoming.

After I sold Roger, I immediately went back to riding Molly. I felt guilty and ashamed that my first horse was a bust. But being back on Molly helped me regain my confidence. At my slightest touch, she knew what I wanted. My heart was full of gratitude for her. It was as if she was telling me, "Look, you can do it. You're doing just fine, and I'm happy to show you the way."

After a couple of months of looking at other horses and toying with the idea of buying a Friesian, my husband said, "I don't know why you don't just buy Molly."

I replied, "Laura would never sell her."

The following lesson was a particularly good one. After we were all done and just chatting while I cooled Molly down, I told Laura the conversation that my husband and I had earlier that week. What she said next took my breath away.

Laura looked me in the eye and said, "I'd sell her to you."

I was stunned. "Really?" I couldn't believe it and needed confirmation she wasn't joking.

Laura chuckled, "She's put in her time as a lesson horse. She deserves her very own person, and it's pretty clear that she loves you. You love each other. You make a great team."

Then we had to talk about money. *Could I swing it?* For a few weeks, I tried to convince my husband to pay for part of the cost, but his response was, "You want her, you pay for her." Could I afford to be her full-time mom? The voice in my head whispered, "what do you want to do?"

On January 6, 2013, I followed my heart and bought my Molly.

She was mine, and I was hers.

All of my childhood dreams didn't even come close to the reality of owning Molly. She was beautiful, elegant, and powerful, with the most expressive face. Still, it was her personality that I loved the most. Every barn visit had me laughing at one of her antics. She *loved* to be groomed, and I loved grooming her.

I spent hours pampering her, trimming the hair around her hooves, giving her baths, braiding her mane. She became known as the best-groomed horse in the barn. Laura would often comment that I'd be worn out before I even started riding when she saw me with two hands on the brush, feet braced against the ground, or making circles as hard as I could with the curry comb as Molly leaned her weight against me.

While I groomed Molly, her neck would lower, her head would turn to the side, and her top lip would stick out as far as she could get it, and I'd laugh. It was that most rare coming together of two souls who recognized and loved each other, flaws and all.

During my time at the barn, Laura told me horror stories of when she first got Molly and how she would try to bite Laura while she was grooming, or how she would go to swing into the saddle and Molly would take off bucking as soon as Laura's right leg left the mounting block. I don't know who *that* horse was, but it wasn't *my* Molly.

I discovered through our relationship that Molly had her own story to tell. A story of a young horse who was brought out into a plowed field after a heavy rain so they could break her. After she freaked out, she was termed unrideable and sold to a cattle guy to be sent to Quebec for slaughter.

When Laura's parents dropped by to deliver a shipment of cattle, her mom, Jean, asked why there was a horse tied out with the cows. She was told Molly was heading to the meat market with the cows. Jean replied, "No, she's not." They paid what the guy would have gotten from the slaughterhouse, and Molly came home to live and learn with Laura. I will be forever grateful that they found her. Their decision to bring her home saved both of our lives.

As I continued to build my relationship with Molly, a whole new world opened up for me. I made friends with good, honest, kind people who loved their horses, loved to be outdoors, loved to ride, and loved to relax and take a breath. Two ladies, in particular, Jackalyn, and Kathy befriended me. We would take our trusty steeds and head out behind the barn, where acres and acres of open fields awaited. Thanks to Molly, I no longer felt like an outsider.

I was finally living my life. I was getting out of the house and interacting with people that I truly liked and who had things in common with me. I was focusing on my own life and enjoying myself for the first time in a very long time. Unfortunately, as things were ramping up in the friend and leisure department, my home life was getting progressively worse. My husband went from complaining that I spent too much time on the couch to complaining that I was out of the house too much. No matter what I did, I couldn't seem to please him.

Sadly, in February of 2015, my life started to crumble when my husband told me he wanted out of our marriage. I did not make him happy, and he needed time to decide what he wanted out of life. In order to do that, he wanted a trial separation. I called Kathy and told her what was going on.

Without hesitation, she told me I could stay with her and her husband Danny for as long as I needed. Kathy took care of me when I couldn't take care of myself; she got me out of bed, and she fed me somewhat forcibly when needed, as I had stopped eating completely. Throughout my struggle, I kept going to work and tried to put on a happy face, but my coworkers knew something was up. I just wasn't up to telling them yet.

At that point, I was still hopeful that my marriage could be saved. I don't know what I would have done without Kathy. I honestly don't know if I'd be writing this today if it wasn't for her. She shared her own story with me, taught me I needed to learn to love myself. She checked on me and made me go and talk to a lawyer so that I knew what my rights were.

After the two-week trial, I went back home. My husband still said he was confused and unsure about what he wanted. He said he needed more time and wanted me to move out. At that moment, I don't know what came over me; I told him if he wanted to leave, it was up to him to do so. He told me I couldn't afford to buy him out of the house, but thanks to meeting with a lawyer, I knew what my rights were. He decided to start looking for a place of his own.

That April, Jackalyn asked if I would like to do a Reiki course called *The Tao of Equus*, which was all about the healing power of horses. I agreed without hesitation. The practitioner's name was Pam, and not only was she a Reiki master, but she also owned a herd of Appaloosas and lived on a farm called Hidden Brook.

This was another life-altering event. I cried a lot during this course. I knew Molly was helping me through this crisis, and I wanted to learn how to strengthen our bond even further. There was so much peace and comfort at Hidden Brook.

At one point, Pam did a little drumming circle, and while I stood there with tears running down my face, the drum got louder and louder. When she stopped, she said, "I started soft with you, but I got louder because you are stronger than you think you are."

I told her I was tired of people telling me I was strong, to which she replied, "If one person says something, it might not mean much, but if multiple people are telling you the same thing . . . maybe it's time to listen."

My husband had purchased a new home and moved out by June of that year. We were officially separated. I was alone in my husband's hometown. I was barely eating or sleeping. It felt like the whole town talked. People I had never met were telling stories about me and my life when they knew nothing about it.

Molly got me out of bed. She made me laugh. She allowed me to cry. She was always happy to see me, but the fear of losing her because I was now a single woman, terrified me. So many questions consumed me. *Should I sell her and make sure she has a good home? What if I moved? Can I find a place for her as well?* I just couldn't face the alternative. I couldn't face another loss. I couldn't lose her too. Molly and the people Molly brought into my life got me through my hardest days.

In September, I met with my ex under the guise of being told we should get together if we wanted to talk about reconciliation. Instead, he told me that he had started seeing someone else. Anxiety took over my body. I started having panic attacks and was having trouble breathing.

I wasn't sure where to turn at first, but Pam's name kept popping into my head. I reached out to her. I told her my situation and asked if she thought she could help. Her response was, "As a matter of fact, I think I can. Reiki can help you through this." We started with three treatments within a three-week period. My breathing and sleeping improved.

Before one of my Reiki treatments, something quite magical happened with Molly. I decided to head to the barn for a quick visit before making the trip to Fredericton. I talked to her and groomed her, and she nickered her low soft nicker that I loved so much.

After grooming, I went to her head and spoke to her. I told her how much I appreciated her, loved her, and how much she had helped me through this terrible time. For a while she stood there with her head in my hands. I held on to her and just allowed myself to feel her, my breath with her breath, one hand on either side of her beautiful head. I kissed her forehead and told her I needed to go, and she lifted her head and started nuzzling my chest.

I smiled and chuckled, but she kept doing it, over and over to the point where I started laughing out loud. I thanked her and stepped back, but she stepped back into me and kept rubbing my chest in the same spot over and over. Remembering I had put an essential oil on that morning, I figured she must have liked the smell. After a while, she stopped and started licking and chewing. I put Molly back in her stall, and I told her I loved her and headed out to my appointment.

On my way, I stopped at a restroom. While washing my hands, I noticed a red spot on my chest and thought it was weird. I was in a rush, so I didn't investigate. As I continued to drive, my chest started to burn and got increasingly hot. I pulled down my visor to peek at the red spot. I was stunned. I had to pull over to the side of the road and get a better look. Was it what I *thought* it was? Pulling my collar down, there it was; a perfectly shaped red heart right above my left breast. Molly had rubbed a heart right over my heart.

Tears poured down my face, and I knew, no matter what happened from here on out, I wasn't alone. Even though I had been cast aside by my husband, I was loved. I knew Molly loved me and would always be there for me. Pure, unconditional, authentic love. Forever and always.

When I told Pam the story, she put her hand over her mouth. She nodded and said, "But she also wants you to know that you have to love yourself too,

Tracey. You are worthy of that."

More tears fell. Molly had deemed me both loved and loveable. Pam asked if I would be ok with her telling this story to her other clients, and of course, I said absolutely! Molly was a teacher, a lesson horse in every sense of the word.

In August of 2018, we attended a clinic put on by Nikki and Mike Porter. During the clinic, there was a series of obstacles that we had to go through, over or on, and it helped to strengthen the trust between horse and rider. At one point, Nikki was asking Molly to move her hip out, but Molly was focused on me. "Oh, she *looooves* you," Nikki said, which made me swell with pride and joy. Nikki saw it too!

At the end of the weekend, we did an obstacle course, and Molly and I received the highest mark Nikki had ever given to a team. Only one point less than a perfect score! I couldn't have been prouder.

Nikki invited me to join her Facebook group called *East Coast Soul Sisters*. Meeting Nikki and having her ask me to join her group led me to write *this* chapter for *this* book and the realization of my dream of becoming a published author. Once again, Molly was the connecting thread to my dreams.

I lost Molly in February of 2021. It still feels like yesterday. The hole that Molly has left in my life is immeasurable. I miss her every hour of the day. She is still with me in spirit. I feel her presence, and I know our love was a once-in-a-lifetime love. She taught me about life, love, respect, friendship, and trust. She introduced me to lifelong friends and always brought the right person into my life at the right time. She taught me how to deal with loss and to lean on others and Molly introduced me to an entirely different world. She showed me how to fly, and I look forward to the day when we will fly again.

About Tracey Gibbons

———

Tracey grew up in a small, picturesque community in Newfoundland where waves lulled her to sleep at night and whales frolicked in the summer. A graphic designer by trade, Tracey loves all things creative and spends her free time painting, baking, and learning more about her newest obsession of pyrography.

While horses were not part of her upbringing, she has loved them all her life and filled her walls with photos and paintings of them as a child. Leaving her beloved Newfoundland behind to make a new life in New Brunswick was a challenge that was made easier when she entered the horse world and fell in love with a little pinto mare named Molly.

Molly changed Tracey's life and made her dream of one day owning a horse a reality. She has seen and felt the impact a horse can make on people's lives. After the loss of her beloved Molly in 2021, her love of horses remains. She is slowly returning to the world of horses, volunteering at horse events, grooming, and hanging out at the barn. Tracey is hopeful that she will find another horse who will teach her in ways no other animal can.

DEDICATION

For Dad who always encouraged me and who loves to spin a yarn; for Mom who loves with all her heart; for Jon, who's love, encouragement, and unwavering belief in me has led me out of the darkest of places; and for Laura, who gave me the most precious of gifts.

BOOK RECOMMENDATIONS

The Gifts of Imperfection by Brené Brown
The Way of the Horse by Linda Kohanov
The Artist's Way by Julia Cameron.

CHAPTER 4
My Adversary

BY TERESA LAFRANCE

SEPTEMBER 5TH, 2020, was one of the most exciting days I've ever experienced. This was the day that my childhood dreams finally came to fruition. After all the years of dreaming, reading every horse book I could get my hands on, watching every horse movie I could find, taking riding lessons as an adult beginner, and after many, many prayers, I finally had a horse of my own.

My heart was so filled with joy, and I felt like it could burst from all the happiness and excitement. Evidently, it showed outwardly as well. As I posed for a picture with my new mare, my smiling husband, exclaimed, "You're beaming!" I stroked her varnished Appaloosa neck and felt joy, peace, excitement, and wonder. I couldn't wait to see what the future would hold for us. Our journey had just begun.

November 6th, 2020, was one of the worst days of my life. That day my eighteen-month-old son Carson went in for surgery to have his right eye removed at The Hospital for Sick Children (SickKids) in Toronto, Canada. Just four days earlier, back home in Alberta, he had been diagnosed with retinoblastoma, a rare form of eye cancer.

The next day we had to fly out to Ontario as he needed to get treatment started as soon as possible to save his life and his left eye. The next few days were a whirlwind as we were flown to the other side of the country, bombarded with incredible amounts of information, and told our son needed immediate surgery. I was on autopilot, doing what had to be done, all the while trying to process what was happening to our little family. I stroked my son's hand as he lay still sleeping from the anesthesia. I felt fear, sadness, and trepidation. I dreaded what the future would hold for us.

These two events in my life, which happened only two months apart, encompassed emotions from opposite ends of the spectrum. If you had asked me when my son was first diagnosed with cancer how these two events would lead me to similar life lessons, I wouldn't have had an answer for you. Looking back now with hindsight, I can answer that question without a doubt.

I have always been a relatively fearful, nervous, and cautious person. I was the kid who never did daredevil stunts for fear of getting hurt. I never threw myself on the ground while playing baseball or floor hockey. I always let the braver kids do those things. I had an extreme fear of dying in my sleep when I was young, and it would take me hours to fall asleep, worrying that I would never wake up.

My aunt died of cancer in her thirties when I was eleven years old. This event left me with a huge fear of cancer. In regard to horses, I have also always been more cautious than most around them. I have too many horror stories in my head of accidents that have happened to people around horses to be anything but cautious. So even though they are my passion, and I enjoy riding and being around horses immensely, there has always been a splash of fear mixed in with love.

Before I bought Xena, my Appaloosa mare, I had been taking lessons for four years. Those were broken-up years as I took breaks when I had my babies and then there were lapses because of some health issues. Eventually, I got to the point that getting my own horse seemed like the best idea to help keep me progressing as a rider, and I had grown a lot in confidence around horses.

After talking with my coach and arranging a boarding agreement with her, I began my hunt for a horse. I tried quite a few, and some I decided against because I could just tell I would feel nervous to ride them on my own. I didn't want to get a horse that I would be nervous to ride as that would defeat the whole point of getting my own horse.

When I tried Xena, she was the only horse I had tried that didn't trigger nervousness. I felt excited and happy when I test-rode her. Before horse shopping, I had prayed and asked God to give me a very specific feeling when I had finally found *the one*. With Xena, I had that feeling.

In my mind it was meant to be, and I went ahead with the purchase. As I said at the beginning of this story, the day I got her, I was ecstatic! I felt so happy and sure of my decision. But lo and behold, my first time riding her as my own would present a reality check.

Nothing crazy happened in that first lesson, but it wasn't great. She tested me a lot and wasn't as easygoing as she had been when I had tried her out. Despite this, I wasn't too discouraged as I knew that we were both going to need time to get to know each other and for her to get used to a new environment.

I rode her once in between lessons and that had gone pretty well. It was after that, during our second lesson together when our downward spiral began. Our second lesson did not go so well. The moment I got on, Xena threw a tantrum, and as I struggled to work through it, she started popping her front feet off the ground.

I was surprised and startled, but with my coach's guidance, I pushed forward and tried to continue on with the lesson. Still she kept doing it. I asked my coach if she could pop on and see if it was a "me" problem or a Xena problem. She got on, and Xena did the same thing but worked through it quicker under my coach's more skilled hands. Unfortunately, this killed any of the confidence I had in her or us as a potential team.

The next few weeks went by, and we continued to struggle. We tried different saddles and pads in an effort to see if Xena's behavior was saddle fit-related. She didn't seem sore, and we were starting to conclude that it was just how she was. She's sassy and smart, and we figured she was testing me as her new rider. Sadly, her smart and sassy ways were making me nervous to ride her, and I was once again confronted by an old adversary: fear.

Fast forward to Monday, October 26th. I read an article online about a mom from the United States who noticed a white glow in her young daughter's eye, which turned out to be a rare childhood cancer of the retina called retinoblastoma. I felt sad for this mother and her daughter and said a small prayer for them when I finished reading the article and then I returned to my life.

Two days later, on Wednesday, October 28th, early in the morning, as I was getting breakfast ready for my kids, I looked down at my eighteen-month-old son Carson and noticed a weird, very faint white-ish shadow in his right pupil. Strange, but it was gone as quickly as it had appeared, so I brushed it off and went about our day.

The white spot on his eye didn't stay away, though. I happened to catch glimpses of it a few more times throughout the day, mostly in low-light situations. I mentioned it to my husband, but he said he couldn't see anything and told me I was being paranoid.

The next day I was keeping an eye out for it, and I saw it a lot more. In one particular instance, I saw what looked like a lumpy white mass with veins in it in his pupil, but as soon as he blinked and looked away, I couldn't see it anymore. Seeing this strange thing in my son's eye made me think of the article I had read. I felt a knot form in my stomach and immediately decided I needed to do something about it.

I arranged an appointment with our eye doctor, which led to Carson getting diagnosed with retinoblastoma by a specialist in Edmonton. Then, being flown to Toronto, where we were told that his best chances of recovery would be to have his right eye removed and then to treat the other small tumors in his left eye with laser and cryotherapy. Everything happened in a whirlwind. We had been flown across the country, leaving our other two children behind with family, been bombarded with an intense amount of information, and then faced with our baby losing his eye.

On November 6th, just four days after being officially diagnosed with cancer, Carson went into surgery to have the enucleation performed. As I waited in the waiting room, holding my husband's hand and praying for our son's surgery to go well, I was once again staring into the ugly face of my adversary: fear.

The same emotion was "running the show" in the two most important areas of my life. I was getting increasingly discouraged with Xena and started to second guess my choice of equine partner. I was frustrated with myself when I felt myself being controlled by my fears, and I desperately didn't want to let that happen. I had dreamed and worked too long to let fear ruin it for me. I was determined to work through it, and my coach was behind me in this decision.

Luckily, we soon discovered a source for some of Xena's negative behaviors. An equine chiropractor said he had no idea how she did it, but she was extremely out of alignment in her withers. He was surprised that the bucking or misbehaving wasn't worse and he said the withers being out of alignment will cause the gentlest, most well-trained of horses to start bucking and acting out because of the pain.

Hearing this allowed some hope to creep into my heart. This meant Xena was actually a very tolerant and patient creature. Maybe once we fixed this and got her feeling better, we just might become the team I dreamed of. Xena would be out of commission for the next three weeks as she would need three adjustments to be back in alignment, and the chiropractor suggested I wait to ride her until they were all done.

Whenever I went to the barn during that time, I just spent time with her. I would groom her and lead her around the arena. I played around with rudimentary liberty, letting her off the lead and seeing what she would do. Off the lead, Xena was a darling. She would follow me around like a puppy, going faster when I would and slowing or stopping whenever I did. Our trust and confidence around each other were growing, and with these, I felt some of the fear slip away.

While the fear started to lessen its hold in my horse life, it was still in full swing in my family life. In January 2021, we were in the middle of Carson's four rounds of preventative systemic chemotherapy treatments.

When we had gotten the pathology results back from his eye that had been removed, it was discovered that the tumor had not left the eye, but it had touched the blood vessels that led to outside of the eye. Because of this, there was no way of knowing if any cancer cells had left the eye and were floating around his body or not. To be safe, we were told that four rounds of preventative systemic chemotherapy would be his best option.

Chemotherapy scared me so much more than his eye removal had. I had to face my cancer fear head-on with this news. I had seen what chemotherapy had done to my aunt's body, and I knew how hard it was on a person. I was terrified of what it could do to my sweet little boy.

It wasn't easy, and we had a lot of bumps along the way. Once he had a couple of rounds of the chemo and was doing pretty well, I started to feel myself relax a bit. Our oncology team was fantastic and always willing to answer questions, and offer support with any worries or concerns I had.

Being on the oncology ward, surrounded by other families and children going through similar things, helped me to feel not so alone. I was finding I could be stronger and braver than I had ever thought possible every time Carson was hooked up for the chemotherapy infusions, or with every port access to draw blood, or every time I cleaned up vomit, or held him as he felt tired and sick from low platelet levels—during everything we had to go through as he received treatment.

I felt all the prayers being said for Carson surrounding us like a blanket through all the graces that God was giving us as we walked this path. What had seemed so impossibly scary just a month before wasn't anymore.

This was just one season of our lives, and when I was able to see the end of this in sight, some of the fear finally slipped away.

As I sat and wrote this, looking at it all in hindsight, I saw the lessons I learned and am continuing to learn through both of these journeys in my life. After receiving the chiropractic treatments, Xena was much better. We made progress and had some great rides. There were a few issues that I eventually concluded were getting in the way of me fully letting go of my fear and that I did not have the time or skills to try and correct on my own.

I recently decided to send Xena to a trainer for a month or two so that a professional could work with her. While she's away, I am taking lessons on one of my coach's horses to gain back my confidence and skills. I am hopeful that when Xena comes home, we will be in a much better position to advance our partnership with more trust and less fear.

Carson is four months post-chemotherapy treatment. He is thriving. His hair grew back, and he's happy and energetic. We have been going to SickKids in Toronto every four to six weeks to continue to have his left eye looked at and to receive laser and or cryotherapy as needed.

As of our last appointment, Carson has not had any new activity for a while, and his doctors have discussed the possibility of extending the time between visits to Toronto because he is doing so well. When this whole cancer journey started, the main feelings were fear of loss and of the unknown. Now I feel hope.

As I reflect, I ask myself how did the situation with Xena help me cope with Carson's cancer, and what did both of these very different situations in my life teach me?

Having my challenges and joys with my horse happening at the same time as Carson's cancer helped me by giving me something else to focus on. Once or twice a week, I was fully able to put all thoughts of cancer, doctor appointments, treatments, and side effects aside and fully focus on my horse and our partnership.

The days I just spent time with Xena gave me peace and joy, even if our other struggles were at the back of my mind. Horses really do have a healing and calming presence. There is something about their eyes, their smell, and their connection with you that have a significant effect on how you view other things going on in your life. As the famous quote by Winston Churchill goes: "There is something about the outside of a horse that is good for the inside of a man."

The two very different situations were able to teach me the same lesson, and it all goes back to the common denominator: fear. In both situations, I had a lot of fear swirling around in my head and heart. Circumstances were out of my control and I wasn't sure how either would turn out.

Unknowns are scary; you have no idea the outcome or what will transpire on the way. We as human beings don't like being vulnerable, and unknowns make us just that. I had let fear rule me many times in my life, and I always felt like I couldn't handle hard things. I never liked looking at my fears in the face as I was worried that somehow I would succumb to them if I did.

The struggle of working through my horse's behaviors and Carson's cancer helped me to remind me that F.E.A.R. has two meanings. Forget Everything And Run, or Face Everything And Rise. We can choose how we handle what is thrown our way in this life, and how we respond can change our life's trajectory.

The choice is ours and ours alone. We must come to these conclusions on our own. We can do it kicking and balking all the way or looking ahead with calm determination.

Fear is a cruel master, it is merciless, and if we don't make up our minds to stand up, we will forever be its slave. I discovered this: When I stood up and faced it head-on, it no longer had power. The fear eventually started to shrink and fade away until I could almost no longer recognize what made me so afraid in the first place.

Throughout these two journeys of horses and cancer, I have learned a lot about myself and what I can do. I have come to realize that I am so much stronger than I ever thought possible. I have learned to trust God more. And I have learned to stand up and face my fears. Aristotle put it best when he wrote: "He who has overcome his fears will truly be free."

About Teresa LaFrance

Teresa is a stay-at-home, homeschooling mom who lives with her husband, three young kids, two cats, a dog, and two chickens in Hinton, Alberta. She grew up on a sheep and cattle farm in Saskatchewan where her love of animals was nurtured. She was the horse-crazy girl who borrowed every horse-related book she could find from the library, and all her dreams as a child were about horses.

She only had the opportunity to get involved in horses as an adult and is currently taking lessons and boards her horse and her kids' pony at her coach's property. She dreams of the day she can own her own property and have her horses at home. Teresa is also an artist who mostly works in pet portraits and is slowly rekindling the long-buried childhood desire to be an author.

Dedication

I dedicate this story to my grandma Valerie, who was the main influence on my love of horses as a child. To my coach Jen, without whom I would not be the horsewoman I am today. She has been an invaluable help to me in my equestrian journey. To my husband Denis, who supports me in all my "horsey" endeavours. To my son Carson, who has shown me how resilient we as humans can be through hard times and how to continue to smile amidst it all. And to God, to whom I am thankful for everything.

Book Recommendations

Hope Rising: Stories from the Ranch of Rescued Dreams - Kim Meeder
Who Moved My Cheese? - Dr Spencer Johnson

CHAPTER 5
STARVED FOR CONNECTION
BY DANIELLE CROWELL

———

I WAS FIRST INTRODUCED to the world of horses when I was eight years old. My best friend started taking riding lessons, and in true best-friend fashion, I started taking them too. What began as an after-school activity to spend more time together quickly became my passion.

I would take a different bus to go to my lesson barn after school, and on the weekends, I would ask my parents to drop me off so I could brush horses, clean stalls, clean tack, and do basically anything to be around the horses. I even went to a week-long summer camp simply because they offered a one-hour riding lesson every day as an activity.

When I was ten or eleven, I was given the opportunity to lease a pony. He was an adorable but naughty little Welsh-cross gelding named Freckles. Freckles taught me some tough lessons of what to do and especially what not to do, like don't attempt to pick out the back hooves when the horse is about to poop. I learned that the hard way.

I joined Pony Club around that time, and Freckles helped bring me through the introductory levels. It was hard when, a year or two later, we competed in our last show and I had to hand the reins over to a new little girl at the end of the day. As kids do around that age, I had a growth spurt. I didn't fit a medium pony anymore, but much to my excitement, my parents and coach had a horse waiting for me.

The first horse I ever *officially* owned was Betty. She was a bay off-the-track Thoroughbred mare with a large star on her forehead. I'd be lying if I said she was the horse I wanted, and I would be lying even more if I said she was the horse I needed. Betty scared me. Like most off-the-track Thoroughbreds, she was fast. She was a kind horse, but she was too forward for me to be riding at that time. We joked that her name should have been Whiplash because she would go from 0 to 60 in a heartbeat.

When I got Betty, I was a confident preteen, but I would often get nervous at the barn. I had started taking riding lessons a few years later than the other girls my age, so they were in a higher level of Pony Club than I was. I always felt like I was behind everyone else. Despite that they were all still riding ponies, competing against other kids. However, because my parents didn't want me to go through the heartache of selling a pony I'd inevitably outgrow, they bought me a horse. So I was now a twelve-year-old on a horse, competing against adults. Suddenly, any form of confidence I had was plummeting with a horse that I was scared to ride.

I spent a few years going further and further down a confidence spiral with Betty. I couldn't compete or even have people watch me ride without bursting into tears because she frightened me. I didn't think I was good enough to be riding her and wished I had a different horse. I wished for many things then: I wished we could afford a different horse; I wished I could control her while jumping; I wished we could naturally find the distance instead of always leaping a stride away and sending me flying. I just wished I could look better in front of everyone else and earn the respect I assumed they didn't have for me.

My parents offered to bring Betty home, and we started clearing the land to make room for her. They saw how much competing was affecting my mental health, and they thought that perhaps if I could just enjoy my time with Betty, rather than focus on competing and advancing in Pony Club levels, I could find the happiness with horses that I once had.

Around this same time, I entered my first relationship. We began dating when we were fourteen, and he went to a different school, so our weekends were consumed with spending time together. His hockey schedule came before my horse schedule, and I began going to the barn less and less.

Although we had a great relationship, the fact remains that when I entered my first relationship with the thought that I wasn't good enough for my hobby, it trickled into feelings of not being good enough for my boyfriend.

Obsessively, I started to compare myself to other girls. I lived in fear that he would leave me for someone prettier. I began compulsively exercising and watching what I was eating, and eventually, it wore me down.

When I was sixteen, I sold Betty and decided I wanted out of horses altogether because my full attention was on my boyfriend. My life at that time was filled with going to the gym, going on social media, and trying to figure out how I could be as pretty as other girls. With my energy being so heavily focused on my appearance, I developed an eating disorder by the time I was seventeen. Within a year, I weighed the same amount as I did when I was ten.

My boyfriend and I broke up a few weeks before we graduated high school. My eating disorder was at its peak and all I wanted to do was push everything out of my life: family, friends, relationships, everything. I didn't want anything positive in my life because I didn't want the nagging feeling that I wasn't good enough for it.

A few months later, through the support of my family and my doctor, I began my journey to get healthy again. I tried many things to make me feel happy again, but unfortunately, with each attempt, I would end up feeling more and more lost.

At this point, my friends had moved away to university while I was still living at home with my parents and working part-time. I lacked a passion for life, and that part-time job was the only thing that made me feel a need to get out of bed in the morning. My heart kept telling me that I needed horses back in my life, but my head wasn't sure I was ready.

I decided to go to university after all, and I enrolled for the winter semester. I started halfway through the year, so there were no frosh week activities to get to know people and I felt like an outsider in the dorms. I eventually made some friends in my hall, and I began partying every weekend. As an eighteen-year-old, it was fun for a few weeks, but that got old pretty quickly.

Once again, I felt lost. I stopped answering my friend's texts, and I started finding excuses to avoid going to parties or meeting up in the cafeteria at supper. Instead, I stayed in my dorm room and started watching Heartland. *Cheesy?* Maybe. But I craved the connection to horses again.

After weeks of being completely disconnected from myself, my friends, and my motivation to be in school in the first place, I made the abrupt decision to leave university. Did I feel like I failed? Yes. Did I feel like I was disappointing people? Absolutely. But I knew it wasn't where I was supposed to be. I moved back home with my parents, got a job, and bought myself a horse. It was time to reclaim my happiness again. It was time to find me again.

Bea, originally named Beauty, was a 14.2 hand palomino Quarter Horse-cross. She wasn't the typical type of horse that I had been drawn to, but she was $800, and that was all I could afford.

When I went to see her with my parents, she was standing in the darkness, tied to a wall in a straight stall. She was obedient and quiet, and we borrowed a trailer and hauled her away a few days later to her new home at a private boarding barn.

The night that we brought her home, I received a phone call from the barn owner asking me to come back to the barn. It was a forty-five-minute drive, but the woman sounded distressed. When my dad and I walked inside, we saw a mean horse. Bea was spinning circles in her stall. She would not allow anyone to go near her. She would lunge over the stall door with teeth bared to anyone who got close and she charged at anyone who dared to open the door.

This was not the horse I thought I bought. Had she been drugged before? I'll never know, but I doubt it. I believe she had what is called "learned helplessness," which is a term for something—animal or human—that suffers from a sense of powerlessness. They are unable to fight, so they shut down and follow orders.

Bea had a newfound sense of freedom in this new home. She had a large box stall, pasture mates, and quality feed. She did not want humans interfering with her again. In the coming days after that, I was asked to take the responsibility of cleaning her stall and leading her to and from her paddock. The barn owner didn't trust her, so I went there—forty-five minutes from home—multiple times a day.

After a few weeks, I had still barely touched my new horse because she was so aggressive. I realized I needed help. Coincidentally, the same day I came to the conclusion I needed to ask for help, I was asked to leave the barn. My horse was too much of a liability with the owner's young kids.

Luckily, my coach allowed us to bring Bea to her boarding barn—the barn I grew up in—to help me out. At our new home, we found the help we needed. We had Bea's teeth floated; they were so long they were hooking and cutting her mouth. Her hooves were trimmed, and we discovered she was suffering from a painful problem called laminitis which was likely masked by the terrible condition of her feet. We got her on a good feeding program and turned her out in a herd.

We let her be a horse and made sure she was feeling the best she could. Bea went from a mean horse who viewed humans with fear and distrust to a bright and happy pony who would come running when I called her in from the field. Her palomino coat went from a dull, off-white color, to a rich gold. I knew I needed horses in my life again to help me heal, but I realized then that Bea had needed me just as much.

While Bea and I were coming together, I was asked to ride a flea-bitten gray Thoroughbred mare named Lizzie to get her in shape so the owners could sell her. Although it was early in our time together, I ended up buying her. It turned out that, to our surprise, Bea was more suitable as a school-horse type, so my coach and I made a trade: She got Bea for the school program, and I got my board for Lizzie paid for.

Just over a year into my partnership with Lizzie, I was presented with the opportunity to move across the country and work at an up-and-coming boarding and event stable in Alberta. I accepted. My job included the typical stable-hand duties, as well as shaping their young homebred Quarter Horses into well-rounded Pony Club-ready mounts to sell.

The days were long, and I was living above the barn. The stable wasn't open to boarders yet and I began to feel increasingly lonely. My negative thoughts started creeping their way back in. I didn't have anyone monitoring what I was eating, so I was restricting myself. I began questioning if I was good enough to train these horses to sell them for a profit, and my negative self-talk became my only friend.

I decided to make it feel more like home, so three months into my new job,

I had Lizzie shipped out to me. Unfortunately, I was so exhausted from the manual labor and not eating enough food to match the amount of energy I was expending that I barely gave her any attention during my off-hours.

One weekend, we had a clinician come to the stable for a groundwork clinic, and I was asked to attend with one of the farm's mares that was for sale. The clinician was also a psychologist, and one evening all the clinic participants gathered in the house to talk about mental blocks. I felt so lonely, vulnerable, and subconsciously craved connection. In tears I spilled the history of my eating disorder and how it was flaring back up again.

As soon as the night came to a close, I felt everyone's energy toward me shift; I felt like they were all watching me. I had people start to bring me food or invite me to lunch and pressure me into getting dessert. I started to become my story again: I was the girl with the eating disorder. I thought they were talking about me: "She's the girl that isn't good enough." I fell back into my downward spiral.

I suddenly wanted to run; I wanted to get away from everything that made me feel like I wasn't good enough. I just wanted to be left alone. I made the rushed decision to put Lizzie up for sale, and she sold quickly. I'll never forget the moment the trailer left the driveway with her inside. As she whinnied inside the steel frame, it felt like my own inner screams of fear, self-hatred, and loneliness were echoing through her.

Shortly after I sold Lizzie, I left my job. I packed up my car and drove myself back across the country toward home. I had an unsettling "now what?" feeling eating away at me because I had met my childhood dream of working on a horse farm, and it hadn't worked out. Where did that leave me?

I struggled to get back on my feet again after moving home. I got a dead-end job that I hated, but I made the best of my spare time by starting a blog about horses and horse care in Nova Scotia. I would stay up until the morning hours working on it and be right back at it again when I woke up.

As that year progressed, things started looking up. For a while I rode the sweetest Thoroughbred/Percheron gelding that will always hold a special place in my heart and I started a new relationship with a man who would one day become my husband. Although my time spent blogging began to decrease, it eventually led me to my first "adult career" working within the digital marketing industry.

To the outside world, things looked good. I was happy, busy, and leading a healthy lifestyle through exercising and healthy food choices, but inside, I was still fighting a battle of loneliness, self-hatred, and perfectionism.

I needed to take my mind off constant calorie counting and picking myself apart, so I decided I wanted a foal to challenge myself with a start-to-finish upbringing. After much searching, I finally found *the one*.

Miley was a medicine hat, APHA filly with bright blue eyes. The medicine hat marking is a horse that is almost entirely white but has a colored patch covering the ears and the top of the head. I was smitten with this odd little girl from the start. However, she was not so smitten with me.

Miley had a stubborn "what's in it for me?" personality. As she grew, we quickly stopped seeing eye-to-eye. We continued to progress with our groundwork, and to an outside eye, it may have seemed like she was a well-behaved filly and like we knew what we were doing, but we butted heads constantly.

I was so frustrated with myself, and it felt like I could never do anything right, so I continued to restrict my eating as a subconscious punishment.

One night, Miley and I were working together, and I was drained of all energy. She was getting away with things that she was too big to get away with safely. I physically couldn't do anything about it. I was exhausted just walking around the ring.

If you don't start taking better care of yourself, your horse could become dangerous. My subconscious voice was loud and clear, as was the message: I needed mental and physical strength to handle Miley safely and to set her up for success. This meant I needed to start taking care of myself so I could take care of her.

I knew where I needed to start, but I was scared. Could I give up my comfort zone of counting calories, reading ingredients, and measuring the scale in order to work with a horse? Was I willing to let the work of helping a horse actually help me?

Before I had time to overthink it, the answer was made for me.

On the sunny afternoon of July 18, 2014, I was crossing the street where I walked every day to get from my apartment to my work. Before I made it across the road, I was hit by an SUV. When I stepped off the sidewalk, I saw the SUV coming from what seemed like far away, but I wrongfully assumed they would see me crossing. I remember in my peripheral vision seeing a large black blur, and then that was it. The impact broke my pelvis in two places and left a large gash on the top of my head.

As I lay in the middle of the street waiting for the ambulance to arrive, I had three thoughts:

First, I heard my coach's voice yelling, "Don't try to get up!" This was a common phrase I recognized from years of falls. If ever there was a time this was important to remember, this was it!

The second thing I thought was, "Well, now how am I supposed to work with my filly?!"

Thirdly, I heard the sobering questions, "What if I died? Would I have been satisfied with the life I've led? Would I have been proud of my choices? Would all of my restrictive habits, stress, and worry be worth it?"

The answer to each question, tragically, was no. I knew this was my wake-up call.

During my recovery, I worked hard every day to re-strengthen my body. While doing that, I began to learn more about myself. I recognized that I am stronger and more resilient than I gave myself credit for. I have taken risks, tried new things, and worked hard. Although things haven't always worked out, I was trying. And that counted for something.

I decided to put Miley into one month of professional training to keep her going. There was no point in both of us being out of work. When I was able to go back to the barn, we progressed together to a point where I was finally proud of us.

I also realized through that experience that although I was proud of our progress, we just were not a true fit for each other—and that was okay! It reminded me that some people, animals, or jobs are not meant to be in our lives forever. Some are here to teach us something, and then it's their time to continue on and teach someone else. I needed to let go of the judgment I felt around selling her. I wasn't "giving up." It was simply time for both of us to move on.

When she turned two and a half years old and was ready for the saddle, I decided to sell her with the agreement that she be professionally started. I'm happy to say she is thriving in a home that loves her to pieces. She's teaching a young girl new things and she will likely have her for the rest of her life, too.

Over the next three years, my life took on many different shapes and forms. I opened a Yoga and Pilates studio since I was so inspired by my own healing and wanted to offer the same to others. I got married, and we bought our first house. My life was going really well, but then that little voice started calling to me again. That time I was more prepared and recognized the pattern.

I called up my coach and asked to start taking riding lessons. It was the middle of January in Nova Scotia, so you know I must have been really aching for horses! She let me ride a stocky green-broke mare and said I was welcome just to come and ride whenever I wanted. After a few months of doing that, I knew I wanted a horse of my own again.

After looking at a few potential options that didn't feel right, my coach approached me about a dark bay Thoroughbred-cross mare. Instantly, I felt a feeling of dread wash over me. She reminded me of Betty. My negative self-talk came back in that instant: "Who am I to be shopping for a new horse? Who am I to want to re-enter the show ring? If I wasn't good enough then, and I won't be now."

I said, "No thanks, that's not what I want," but what I was really saying was, I don't want to go back to that place in my head again.

As if she could read my mind, her response was, "Hear me out. She's nothing like Betty." I hemmed and hawed because, similar to Betty, she wasn't the horse that I wanted, but at that moment, little did I know that, unlike Betty, she'd be the horse that I needed.

I finally ended up trying the horse named Minnesota, lovingly known as "Sota," on Good Friday in March of 2018. She was a four-year-old Thoroughbred-cross mare with no markings and was such a dark bay that she looked black. I swung my leg over her back, and off we went. I'll never forget that first ride. I wished her canter would never end, and she safely took me over fences.

Unbeknownst to her, it was my first time jumping again in about seven years. She was sold on the spot. That Good Friday became the best Friday, one that would lead me into a deeper relationship with myself and ultimately change the course of my life forever.

That summer, Sota brought me back into the show ring. We went to a jumper training show and placed third in our division. I was wearing my old Pony Club polo shirt that was about fifteen years old, an old pair of hand-me-down breeches, half-chaps that kept unzipping, and—gasp!—a black bridle that I borrowed from my coach to use with my brown saddle.

Normally, I'd be feeling self-conscious of the fact that I wasn't decked out in all the fancy gear, but on that day, with that horse, you couldn't wipe the smile off my face if you tried. It wasn't about other people anymore. It wasn't about their judgment and my need to hide from it. It was about my joy and our connection.

That winter, I decided to move us to a new boarding stable closer to my house. It was a boarding-only barn with no dedicated coach or lesson program; you bring in your own trainer if you want to take lessons. It was a little nerve-racking to leave the support of my coach, but I was excited for the opportunity to be at an adult barn, have a healthy mix of trails and rings to ride in and be surrounded by a variety of disciplines to learn from. And learn I did.

Soon after arriving, Sota started getting cranky to brush and tack up. She was lashing out while in the cross ties and stall and was unwilling to do much under saddle. I thought she should be assessed by a professional, so I had my vet come take a look at her. After his assessment, he diagnosed her with quite severe stomach ulcers.

After being treated for ulcers, Sota was still "off." She was hard to handle, anxious and flighty, and difficult to ride. She was physically developing well, but her mind was going in a different direction. My sweet horse was becoming anxious and pushy.

One winter day, I went to ride in the indoor arena and Sota's paddock mate also happened to be in the ring. We were walking along very tensely, and suddenly that horse and rider picked up the canter right behind us. Sota reared, bolted, and then proceeded to buck me off.

I was caught off guard when she reared, and I went flying backward. The woman in the ring told me that she was relieved when I fell off because she thought Sota was going to flip over on top of me. Apparently, when she reared, my head was just a few feet from the ground.

Suddenly, I went back to that twelve-year-old girl. I was scared of my horse again. Only this time, I knew I needed to seek support rather than hide.

That experience started a journey for my horse and me to learn more about each other. We took riding and groundwork lessons with a variety of instructors. I had a few scary trail rides and a lot of scary times in both the ring and the stall because we didn't yet trust each other.

I considered going back to my coach's barn more times than I could count, but I knew I would never develop my true horsemanship skills if I always relied on someone else to give me the answers. I started asking this question: "Why did she suddenly change when we moved?"

I discovered the barn I moved to was filled with experienced riders and their talented horses. I wanted to be like them, and I wanted to look good in their eyes. I outfitted myself and my horse to look like we knew what we were doing, but when it came time to actually go into the ring, I would avoid that area if anyone else was already in there. I didn't want them to see us struggling. I didn't want them to look down on me.

What changed when we moved was *me*. I started doubting myself and Sota knew it. I was letting my fear of judgment steal my confidence in both of us.

In yoga, we're taught to be mindful of our bodies and our breath. We're taught to be aware of when our mind starts drifting and how that affects our bodies. We're also taught to be aware of our body and how our posture affects our minds, but there was a disconnect between my centered, mindful self who practiced yoga and the self I was with my horse.

At the barn, I did everything that I was taught not to do; I had negative thoughts starting from the moment I drove up the barn's driveway. I kept my body tense, moved anxiously, and breathed from my chest in short, shallow breaths. My horse read me like a book, and she didn't want anything to do with me until I calmed down. I craved horses for their connection, but my horse was teaching me that I didn't yet have the most important connection of all: my connection to myself.

One day, I had a groundwork lesson with a friend who's an extremely talented and professional trainer. She very kindly, yet firmly, told me that Sota acted the way she did because she viewed me as a liability. She felt my fear and anxiety, and she didn't trust that I was capable of being the leader. So, she stepped in as the leader—which we often view as pushy and disrespectful—because she knew I didn't believe in myself.

Once I had that breakthrough, and once I started to allow myself to let down my guard—to breathe, slow down, be conscious of my thoughts, and be aware of my body—everything with us changed.

Sota became more relaxed and playful again, and because of her, I started to believe in myself. Finally, she forced me to begin to be the best version of myself. She's still a saucy mare, but she's given me the confidence to want to do better, to keep going, and to try harder throughout our journey. If I hadn't learned that, I might have given up.

Through our time together, she's helped to make me feel good about myself by showing me what I'm capable of. I've healed from my eating disorder because I recognize my triggers and know that my value is more than how much I weigh. And because of this, I've completely changed my life to be better than I ever imagined possible, both personally and professionally. As my trainer friend said, "This horse is going to force you to level up and be the best version of yourself. She won't take anything less."

In just three and a half years of having Sota in my life, we have been through more ups and downs to count, and I still have so much to learn because she still has so much to teach me. I call her my greatest yoga teacher. When I don't feel like I'm good enough and I have those negative thoughts creeping back in, she forces me to overcome them and to make myself good enough.

I will forever be grateful for each horse's lessons, but I will never forget the lessons that Sota continues to teach me. Thank you, Minnesota, for teaching me the greatest lesson of all: I am capable of more than I think. I just have to believe in myself.

About Danielle Crowell

Danielle has been involved with horses for over two decades and currently has two special horses in her life, her mare Sota and her gelding Paco. Danielle credits a lot of the healing from her eating disorder to horses and has since become an advocate for mental health and body image. She has worked with multiple non-profit organizations to help young girls build their self-esteem and Danielle owned a yoga studio that focused on building positive body image and self-love with the tagline: *"Find Solace Within."*

Danielle is now enjoying a quiet(er) life with her horses, dog, and husband as they build their dream property in the woods of Nova Scotia.

Dedication

This chapter is dedicated to my parents, Lorraine and Brenton, for having no idea what they were getting into when they took me for my first riding lessons and unwaveringly supported me through it all. Thank you for working tirelessly to give me everything.

To my coach since the start, Suzanne, you have been a mentor to me from the very beginning. I am proud to call you not only my coach but also my friend.

To my husband Mike, who has always supported my dreams and follows me in my wildness. I'll love you forever.

And finally, to all the horses who have impacted my life, thank you. I am sorry if I haven't given all of you everything you deserved. Now that I know better, I'm committed to doing better.

Book Recommendations

Untamed by Glennon Doyle
Women Who Run with The Wolves by Clarissa Pinkola Estes
The Happiness Project by Gretchen Rubin
Big Magic by Elizabeth Gilbert

CHAPTER 6
BEFORE AND AFTERS

BY AMBER HOLM

———

I STOOD SEVERAL FEET away from a young wild horse that I could not touch. A wild horse that I had been reaching out to for so many hours that the hours had added up to months. In this style of permission-based mustang gentling, we begin gaining the trust of the young horses in a 12 x 12-foot square pen constructed out of panels high enough to keep a wild horse safe.

I had spent most of the cold Oregon winter in this gentling pen, bundled up, and determined to learn this new-to-me-skill. At that point, wild mustang gentling seemed more like a myth or an art or a gift than something I could do. Perhaps it was a gift I did not possess. I shivered and began to wonder if I would ever get to touch this horse.

She was a dun filly with a sturdy build. She had a golden-buttery coat and pronounced primitive markings down her back and legs. River, as I called her from the first moment I saw her, was an orphan fresh off the Warm Springs Native American Reservation. She was not a horse born into domestic privilege. Before her time with me, River ran with her family band in their high desert home. Western desert lands are so rugged, open, and honest that I often wonder how the sagebrush can survive there, never mind horses or even humans.

In her eyes, soft and wide, I could see River's Spanish ancestors and the wild horses of the West running free. With my right hand, I reached out for her again. She measured up her escape route through the corner of the pen and I read the fear in her eyes and noted her quivering shoulder. I felt her pain of being taken from her wild lands, her family band, and her mother course through me. And then I felt my own pain. Tears flowed, streaming down my face, cutting the dirt on my cheeks like a desert river. Without any control or thought, I cried out, "Where are you?"

I grew up an East Coast equestrian. My love for horses came when I was young and was encouraged by my mother, who shared the same love of all animals, really. In the beginning, I spent hours riding my horse down the white sandy roads that surrounded my childhood home. Wild and bareback, with a gang of other bikini-clad horse girls, we would leave the house in the morning for a day full of galloping and swimming and then return, hungry and sunburned, with our horses before dark. They were the purest of horse days.

My mother always had the vision, having the uncanny ability to select beautiful horses, and I, with my steady hand and hours spent in the barn, had the skill. With a budget far less than my Palm Beach equestrian counterparts, she and I grew into a passionate dressage team. I spent my middle and high school years hanging on white vinyl fences, pining after imported dressage warmbloods that we could not afford to buy. My "Momager" and I made do with horses that were pretty and sweet, more than expensive and flashy. I often won in competitions, and I learned a practical version of horsewomanship that served me well at the time.

I tend to organize life in a chronicle order of before and afters: before marriage, after marriage, before kids, after kids, before my mother was killed, and after my mother was killed.

It was notable the way the pretty light played that afternoon. It was a sunny November day in an often cloudy Portland. I glanced at the sunbeams as they danced through the blinds on the blonde-colored hardwood floor. My eyes floated upward to see the sheriff's car in the driveway. I was mid-phone call with my best friend and told her I would call her back before I slipped the phone into my pocket.

A young deputy asked if I was Amber Trono. I sheepishly nodded. "Well, I used to be." No one had called me that since before I was married. A teenage version of me suddenly wondered if I were in trouble for something: A court order? Did I forget to pay a parking ticket? I felt bad for the green officer. He must have drawn the short straw in what I thought was daily disciplinary duty.

His voice cracked, "Do you know Kimberly Gray? I'm sorry to tell you she has died." That is all he knew. My knees could not support me.

That pretty November light vanished.

My mother was killed by her partner in a domestic murder-suicide. There is much of the following days and months that I do not remember. Yet, so many of the nuances are still vibrant.

I forget the plane ride to my hometown in Florida but can remember signing my mom's cremation order before I boarded the plane. I forget the neighbors' faces but can still see the chrysanthemums someone placed below the yellow crime scene tape blocking the front door. I forget how I hastily packed my mom's things but will never forget the gruesome details of the crime scene. I forget, a week later, returning to motherhood, but I recall, a month later, saying to my best friend that I did not know how I would survive the piercing pain within me.

In the early months of grief, I realized that I could not live there anymore, on the west side of the Cascades, in that lush Oregon valley. It felt like the Valley of The Shadow of Death. I had lost my soul-horse to colic there and had lost my mother. Now I was scared I was losing myself there too. It was time for my family to go back, back to the last place I remember things to be good, back to the High Desert.

The much-needed space to heal was ample in the arid High Desert. "There is more room here, on the east side of the Cascades. Room for more horses. The mountains are healing. They have room here, too. More acreage will do. Yes, this is where the healing will happen. The light can return here," I told myself out loud, grief and gut leading what felt like my survival mission.

Living on the dry side of the Oregon Cascades, with the space to heal, the slow returning light, and more land, it seemed logical that I volunteer to foster for a local rescue that had tugged at my heartstrings in one of their fundraising videos.

This particular video showed horses in body condition that I had never seen before, and the music accompanying the video melted me into a puddle of tears. For me, the video highlighted my ignorance about an animal that I thought I already knew how to love. I had to know the people who did this work. I had to learn *how* the people that did this were able to do this heart-wrenching work. I had to be a part of this.

Here is where I should admit, into adulthood, I was rather ignorant to horse rescue, never mind any real knowledge of the wild mustangs. To me, most horses were well cared for, and the mustangs were an American legend and Western folklore, not an animal that was enduring long-lasting strife.

Two weeks after seeing that fundraising video, on a cold Christmas Eve, we had our first foster horses: two wild mustangs the rescue had pulled from the kill-pens. I still did not really know what a wild mustang was, but I was there to feed and water this beautifully moving gray mare and her smaller, very shy bay companion. One foster horse led to another, and then to several foster horses, which led to more involvement with the horse rescue until I measured my life in yet another before and after: my life before horse rescue and my life with horse rescue.

In the American West, there are generally two or so types of wild mustangs. The wild horses that live on Bureau of Land Management land and the horses that live on Native American Reservation land. The United States Federal Government manages the former, and the latter is governed by the laws and tribal councils of the sovereign nations. Both types of these horses, BLM or Reservation, face round-up, depressing holding-pens, and often end up in the slaughter pipeline and being shipped for horse meat export.

Wild mustang horses live in bands: families of horses that may include a lead stallion, some low-ranking bachelors, the mares, and their offspring. A mare may have a baby at her side but still travel with her yearling from the previous year. Some fillies may stay in the band with their mother for a lifetime. Horses are sold to slaughter by the pound, so babies are separated from their slaughter-bound mothers and family members.

Be it by land management practices or an income source, these horses are taken from their wildlands and their entire family. Rescues like 3 Sisters Equine Refuge step in between the BLM overflowing holding pens or Tribal members and the slaughter pipeline to nurture, gentle, and responsibly place these mustangs with forever guardians.

For the first few years of fostering rescue horses, I mostly took care of elderly, misused, and thrown-away horses that had been saved from auctions where animals were often priced too low are swooped up by meat buyers. It was into my third year of fostering when Cyndi, the president and founder of the horse rescue—and my dear friend—agreed to let me foster two young fillies that had just been brought in from the Warm Springs Native American Reservation. Cute baby horses sounded like a good idea. I mean, how wild could they be?

They were small. Their ribs were showing. They were full of worms, and they were scared. Tucked into the corner of the pen, the dun horse hid behind a pretty chestnut. Neither horse looked older than six months; neither horse had been handled by humans, at least not in a positive way; and neither horse knew they were about to fold into domestic life. Luna and her herd mate, River, came to my pastures for some healing.

After they'd had some time to settle in, gaining weight and better health, it dawned on me that these young horses needed to be domesticated. Full disclosure here: I think that my wild horse naive self believed that—or at least unrealistically hoped that—if I fed them well and often, these wild mustang fillies would eventually come around and just slip into a halter. Where then, I would welcome them with open arms to their shiny new domesticated lives.

I was wrong. These young mustangs needed to be gentled. And I was the one that needed to do it.

The rescue has a trainer that specializes in gentling horses. I had never really thought to enlist the help of such a trainer, as I had been a horsewoman most of my life.

How hard could gentling a couple of fillies be?

I could not even get them into a pen, at least not with less than a half of a day spent chasing and herding them around their half-acre pasture. As it turns out, wild mustang training is extremely rewarding work, but not the same as working with a domestic horse. I called the trainer.

Katie is a horse whisperer of sorts, although she would likely shy away from the title and even commentary about her life-changing impact on the horses, and humans that she touches. Before we began our training, Katie warned me in a casual but heartfelt way about how wild horse gentling changed her and her horsemanship. A competitive eventer and lifelong equestrian of several disciplines, she explained how her heart work was with these wild horses. I understood her point on some level, given my previous dressage life, but in hindsight, I think Katie saw something about to happen that I did not, something within me.

Luna, the beautiful chestnut filly with a flaxen mane and tail that came in from the Reservation with River, had been a model for the ease that some mustangs can offer a beginner gentler. Within a few sessions, I was able to tote her around by her colorful yearling halter and marveled at my newfound skill. I was a horse-rescuing, mustang gentler extraordinaire!

Beginner's luck.

A couple of months into our training and four years past my mother's death, there I stood, where I had been standing for countless hours, in the wintery cold of a 12 x 12-foot gentling pen, reaching out to River who would not reach back. River, with her wide, kind eyes, remained safe but heavily guarded.

At one point, I considered hiring Katie to just gentle River.

Quitter, I thought.

Instead, during our lessons, Katie stood on the outside of the pen, guiding my body position, eye contact, lack of eye contact, pressure and release, and critiquing my use of the kind tools of the gentling discipline.

It was on that particular night, months into my training, that I left the gentling pen alone, defeated and crying out for my mother's help. My instincts told me that my time to finally touch River would be soon, but not that night.

After my tearful plea, while walking back to the barn, I understood that touching this horse, touching any wild horse for that matter, would take some reconciliation on my part with the person for whom I was pleading to come forward.

"Where are you?" reverberated through me again.

I asked myself the hard questions that night: Why did those words come pouring out of me without control? Why, standing there with that horse, did I yearn for my mom? Was it her that I really yearned for? How did I get here, doing this work with these horses? Am I meant to do this work? And why did I not think I was worthy enough to touch this wild creature? Broken open to the pain of grief for the loss of my mother that I carried with me, the work that I needed to continue doing, and the insight on how far I had come, I cried a lot of tears.

I realized the skill that I needed to touch this seemingly untouchable filly was right in front of me; I had to show up as my authentic, imperfect, and healing self when I worked with this horse. And, if I could do that, River would meet me in that place as a stunning, mirror-to-my-soul.

While that night was for reflection and crying and grieving, the next day was for learning and implementation. I always knew that for a horsewoman, a horse could be a mirror to the soul. What River and this process were teaching me was that a wild horse, with their keen instincts still intact, could magnify that mirror one thousand times over.

With a mustang in a pen where safety for both horse and human are of the utmost priority, there is no room for anything but showing up as one's authentic self. Ego and pride need to be left behind, not only for safety but because these horses can swiftly see past defenses that render a human powerless.

A wild horse does not live in the future; they do not lament in the past; their survival depends solely on the present. Being present, honest, unguarded, and with heart cracked wide open for these wild horses allows for a cadence through the whole human body. It is in this flowing rhythm that a mustang finds ultimate trust. Stoic, guarded, and stiff has no place here, not with these beings.

That night I had called out for my mother, the woman who planted then

63

nurtured my love for horses. With these wild mustangs, I had to know that my mother was keeping me safe. I wanted her to see my work with the rescue and the wild horses that were so far from where I had come from. In that pen, digging deeply for understanding, self-love, and forgiveness, my untamed, horse-loving heart missed my mom terribly. I wanted her there with me. I had not let myself admit that in so long. Simply put, I was a horse-crazy girl that missed her mom.

I also came to understand that I was also crying out for myself.

Where are you now?

I was asking my true self to come forward. I was asking for her to accept the stages of grief and not always be so strong. I was crying for her to find herself capable of doing this work. I was crying for her to let go of life's happenings that led her to this work. I was asking for my true self to know that she could do hard things. That she could let her guard down and that she was worthy of touching this beautiful horse.

I cried for River, too, her big dark eyes, so forgiving but scared.

Where are you?

I cried out for the fear she must have had leaving her band and her ancestors' desert lands. On her behalf, I cried for the fate of her family. And I cried for her future, knowing the life that I could offer her. I cried because she, too, lost her mother.

Present. Honest. Unguarded. Heart wide open. Flowing perfectly through the pulses of my imperfection, that next day, after all the night's pleas and tears, was the day that I first touched River.

In the High Desert, on most days, the pretty light returns to my life. My family lives in the shadow of the majestic Cascade Mountains, among the domestic horses, elderly foster horses, and several wild ones, totaling over twenty sentient beings. Of course, River and Luna are here too, stunning as ever, learning and teaching as they continue to settle into domestic life, and I continue to honor their wild roots.

I have softened to the evolving version of me, "after my mother was killed," and "my life with horse rescue." Some days, with my own band of warrior-horse-rescue women, including Cyndi and Katie, we must act swiftly to save an abused elderly horse's life. Other days we return to the reservation or holding pens to pick up whatever pieces of a mustang family band that we can save, feeling drained and defeated as we leave countless behind. On the best of days, we look into the eyes of a horse that is safe and celebrate our victories.

Katie, the horse whisperer, was right. I am forever changed by the wild ones. As I continue to be a student of these horses and learn how to work with and for them, they are present in every part of my life. While I will always carry that part of me, long gone are the days of the East Coast horsewoman that I once was.

Now, I work every day for the presence, self-love, understanding, and heart that these wild mustang's command: not to be just a horsewoman but a better Woman-Of-The-Horse.

It was during those hours with River that I came to deeply understand that every event in my life, even, and maybe especially, my mother's death, brought me right here, to this exact place; authentic, with heart cracked wide open—right where I need to be.

65

About Amber Holm

Amber rode her first horse when she was six while on a dude-ranch-type trail ride during a trip to Oregon. She was hooked. Growing up in South Florida, Amber took guardianship of her first horse by the age of ten. Trail riding, hunter-jumper shows, and dressage shows took up much of her youth.

Career, family, and life events brought Amber to central Oregon, where she lives with her family, raising three young men on a ranch full of horses. Most of the horses on Varekai Ranch are rescue equines ranging from rehab to wild mustangs.

All of the horses are saved by the rescue 3 Sisters Equine Refuge that Amber works with. Amber is currently training to be a certified Reach Out to Horses trainer, which is a method of horsemanship and wild horse gentling based on the language of the horse. It is her hope to support the wild horses that are displaced by providing a gentle transition into domestication, honoring the mustang, an American legend, and helping to save one horse at a time.

Dedication

To my mom, Kimberly, and all the other wild angels that watch over us

66

and keep us safe as we dance with the beautiful horses.

Book Recommendations

Wild Horse Country: The History, Myth, and Future of the Mustang, America's Horse by David Philips
Desert Chrome: Water, a Woman and Wild Horses in the West by Kathryn Wilder
Escaping Tradition: Discovering the Next Generation of Horsemanship by Anna Twinney and co-authors

CHAPTER 7
SPIEGEL

BY ANTONIA FELDKAMP

—

SINCE I WAS a little girl, I have been around horses and was trained in classical dressage and show jumping. I have trained in a racing stable, spent time on wonderful trail rides on western horses, driven carriages, participated in competitions, and spent most of my teens in a local horse club.

Throughout that, what has fascinated me the most has always been horsemanship. I read a lot about it but never had the courage to pursue it, partially due to lack of opportunity and partially due to lack of bravery required to be different from the horse people around me.

Like with many topics of interest in my life, I forgot about horsemanship for years, but after some time, it came back to me. It was with Pepsi that I finally began to study it.

Pepsi and I commenced our journey together when she was fourteen years old. She was a Hanoverian dressage horse, and I was one of three ladies riding and taking care of her. During those five and a half years, Pepsi and I formed an incredible team. I became great friends with Pepsi's owner and the other horsewomen at the stable during that time. When I left my home at the end of 2019 and needed to say goodbye to Pepsi, she was one of my closest friends and my soul mirror. She reflected an authentic me like no other.

Amongst all my horse friends, she is the one who taught me to interact with horses consciously.

Pepsi and I started to grow together as a team in the spring of 2014. I rode her six to seven times a month and was mainly asked to ride her out as the others trained dressage. We got to know each other well during that time. Looking back now, I see that our relationship was quite superficial—though I was unaware of it.

When Pepsi's owner gave birth to her first child, I offered to take care of her for three months. Pepsi lived with a group of horses, and most of the time, when I came to see her, she would be standing in her field. I always had trouble catching Pepsi, until one day, she started coming to me when I called her name.

I realized our connection was deepening, and I felt pride when she started to listen to me more. Even though those months started fostering our relationship, I did not fully see the beauty of her opening up to me then.

In 2015, I began to meditate and learned a lot about my inner self and my emotions. I started to feel how blocked I was in many ways. To that point, I was a master in locking everything away if it threatened to touch me too deeply. I had always loved horses and had connections with them, but never was I able to open up my heart to them completely, nor any other creature.

Because of my inner work, I discovered that Pepsi was way ahead of me in terms of opening up. Her coming to see me when I called her, working hard during lessons, or walking by scary things during our hacks outs were her ways to show up for me. After I finally realized this, I remember how sorry I felt that I had not seen it sooner.

Me, the big horse lover, who had always thought I had such a good connection with horses, had overlooked so many signs and gifts. It took a while to forgive myself and completely let go of my old patterns but I opened up more to Pepsi after that.

In time, Pepsi and I started to develop our very own flow. I stopped coming to her stable stressed out from the day and forcing both of us to do what I had typically done with a horse. Instead, I started to listen to myself and to her to figure out how we both could have a nice time.

When we rode out, we chose the pace together. If she was tired, we would only stroll around at a walk. When she was lively and overflowing with energy, I chose ways to give us the opportunity to trot and canter more. Strangely enough, most of the time, our moods were identical.

In addition to riding, we also started to collect wild herbs together. I have been interested in herbs for years, and one day we crossed a little grove with a lot of wild garlic. I intuitively dismounted and wanted to pick some leaves. Pepsi, on the other hand, didn't like my decision. She became impatient and pranced around me. I ended up picking only two or three leaves before I decided that it wouldn't work like that. I wanted to be able to get off her back and collect herbs, but I also wanted her to be comfortable with the situation.

So, in the following weeks, we rode to places where I knew herbs would grow, but also where she would have the opportunity to graze. Before I started to pick anything, I made sure she was comfortable where we were.

After a couple of times, her behavior changed, and while I was busy with the herbs, she would graze or wait quietly. She became so patient that I could even use her height to collect elderberries later in the year. She had turned into a wonderful herbal witch horse during that summer. When she saw me binding my herbal bag onto the saddle, I think she knew this meant that she would get some extra food. And I was happy to have a friend on my herb-collecting adventures.

As our time together progressed, I learned more about horsemanship which allowed us to better understand each other. Two trainers from our stable asked if I would be interested in joining a group to learn about groundwork. I was very excited, but if you asked Pepsi, I am not sure how much she appreciated me pushing her into this at the beginning.

The other horses stressed her out, and as most of the group were new to learning about groundwork, like I was, we spent a lot of time standing around, watching and listening to the trainers.

I started to learn how to read Pepsi's body language and use my body to communicate with her consciously. She would get upset if certain horses came too close to us. She would prance around and push me. I tried my best to help her relax and make her feel comfortable as I felt those tools were part of my path to connect with her and myself. I asked people to keep their distance from us, trained in empty corners of the arena, and sometimes, when she had done an excellent job, just left the lesson early.

Over time, she got more laid-back, and I could focus on myself more. I learned that whatever I felt or thought was communicated to Pepsi through my body language. I had taken management training about body language, and my mind technically knew about it, but it was only through the groundwork with Pepsi I truly understood it.

When I asked Pepsi to walk on the right hand, she'd nearly always do nothing. In my old mindset, I would have been mad at her because she did not do what I had asked her to do. After improving my understanding of how to communicate clearly, I immediately checked myself to see if I caused her to react.

With the help of the trainers, we figured out I was sending contradictory signals. When I asked her to move to the right, I, for some reason, always made a step in the right direction, positioning myself a little in front of her. So for her, on the one hand, asking her to stay where she was, and on the other hand, asking her to start walking. She mirrored it by doing nothing but looked at me with question marks in her eyes.

After I understood what was going on, I watched myself closely when I asked Pepsi to start walking toward the right. *Voilà*, she started to walk. I was so happy when it worked out for the first time and thankful to her for showing me that just because I think I said something does not mean I actually did or that I was clear in saying it. Learning from her how to watch my own posture, gestures, or the intonation of my voice was way more effective for me than any training my employer had paid for. Now Pepsi was the perfect mirror giving me honest and direct feedback.

My new horsemanship skills and understanding from many meditations were soon able to transfer into everyday life. I was able to use these skills when I went into a meeting I felt insecure about. I took a few minutes before each event, remembering a moment of insecurity with Pepsi and what helped us in the situation.

Over time, my body automatically adapted the patterns it had learned with her. I was able to relax my breath. I sensed which energy I was in at the moment. I adjusted my posture and made clear to myself what I wanted to achieve. Previously, I would have walked into the meeting acting cool and rational to cover my insecurities.

I was then able to walk in grounded, still feeling nervous, but with a smile on my face and a mindset of trust in myself. If I could handle a thousand-pound horse with the smallest signals, I could handle a bunch of managers, too. Instead of feeling frozen, I stood more relaxed and vibrant and felt way less inner pressure. Without this pressure, the whole atmosphere of such events became lighter and less anxiety-provoking for me.

Another skill I acquired was setting clear boundaries and saying "no," rather than giving in to others easily when I was uncomfortable. Through the work with Pepsi, I had learned that a friendly but determined "no" is more likely to be accepted than a "no" spoken out in fear or pure self-protection.

As Pepsi and I continued our new work together, another thing changed. We both began to trust more. I will never forget how, during one training session, Pepsi stood beside me, dropped her head, and I started cuddling her between her ears. While I was happy and astonished at the same time, one of the trainers came and said, "Oh wow, she really trusts you." I must have looked at her quite confused as she started laughing and explained to me what Pepsi's posture meant.

Pepsi hated her head being touched, especially between her ears. That was a defining, heart-opening moment. I felt how deep our connection had become as she stood there in the middle of the arena with all the other horses around, and instead of being stressed, she allowed me to touch her. After learning this, I felt incredibly thankful. Since then, I have tried to watch my feelings closely every time I am around horses because I know that doing so helps me to understand myself and reflect what my horse might sense. They have become my mirrors, and Pepsi has taught me how to look into them.

The next step for Pepsi and me was to take our dressage to the higher level. To be honest, I have never been a great dressage rider; I had never seen a lot of sense in it. I found it very boring. In my youth, showjumping and trail riding had been way more attractive to me than simple dressage.

Simple dressage, ha!

Now, dressage is as much talking to my horse for me as groundwork is. When I saw other horsemen and horsewomen riding their horses bareback and with only a neck rope, I felt in my heart that I would like to be able to communicate with horses in this way. I talked to Pepsi's owner and our trainer, who both liked the idea and agreed to me starting to ride with a neck rope during lessons.

Luckily for me, Pepsi had been trained with a neck rope already from one of her former riders. Our trainer had taught us classical dressage training and showed me how to ride Pepsi properly so we would both use our bodies correctly. Pepsi and I had a good starting point for the neck-rope adventure.

I borrowed a neck strap from a fellow rider and was super excited for our first neck-rope lesson until my trainer said, "I thought you wanted to ride with the neck rope. What's the bridle doing on her head?"

I had thought we would still use the bridle as a safety backup in the first neck-rope lessons, but this was not to be the case. When my trainer took the bridle off, I became incredibly nervous. Sitting on Pepsi on a cool autumn day, having nothing in my hand to stop her if she took off, frightened me deeply.

Despite my fear, I forced myself to remember how strong our connection had become over the last few months, and I convinced myself to trust her. I leaned forward toward her head and said something like, "Pepsi, I am scared as hell and am not trusting myself with this, so please be good and gentle with me. I trust you."

Pepsi was wonderful and patiently allowed me to get used to the neck rope. I was glad that no one else was in the arena with us as it started off quite chaotic. Even though she seemed to be a bit irritated herself by the changed conditions, Pepsi stayed gentle and calm during the first lessons. She clearly mirrored me and how I was consciously using my body to ride.

I am thankful for my trainer, who knew both of us well enough to help me understand when it was me not using my body correctly or Pepsi ignoring me in the high hopes to avoid work. Over time, we worked through regular dressage movements with the neck strap: rhythm, collection, lateral movements, leg yielding, haunches in and out, and counter canter. Our trainer had no mercy and kept telling me that many good riders regularly train with only a neck rope, so I had no excuse if something did not work out.

As I now had been forced to use my body more intensely than before, I benefited from all the time I spent with Yoga, Qi Gong, and Body Meditations. I already had a good feeling for my body, making it easier to sense what I was doing on horseback. I realized how stiff I was in my hips and how often I blocked Pepsi in her natural movement.

When I rode out with a friend, she only used a riding pad instead of a saddle. We started talking about the difference between both. Following my gut feeling, I replaced the saddle with a riding pad from then on. Again, I was putting aside a fear that a saddle was so much safer than a simple pad.

It worked out wonderfully. I felt Pepsi's movements much better, and with my legs hanging in a more natural posture, the tension in my hips reduced automatically. Pepsi's flow, combined with relaxing breathing exercises, helped me open up my hips.

I had problems with my sacroiliac joint for a long time and needed to regularly see my Dorn Therapist to unblock it. After I learned to take up the energy of Pepsi's body, the intervals between my therapy sessions became longer. Finally, I got to the point that if I felt that my joint started to block, I could help myself with specific exercises and hardly needed to see a therapist for that anymore.

Before ending my story, I would like to share one of my most precious moments with Pepsi. We were participating in a skill game trail at the Christmas celebration at our stable. It was a cold winter day, and we had an audience. I was confronted with my old fear of riding with a neck rope once again. Luckily, my trainer gave me enough self-confidence that I could give it a try. We rocked it! While Pepsi was a little nervous, I was super enthusiastic to ride the trail course.

When the starting signal was given, I felt Pepsi begin to shy back from all the obstacles in front of us. I also felt my heart jump, as I wanted to have fun and do this together. My wonderful Pepsi followed my lead. She was with me, and in the end it did not matter whether we had a neck rope or a bridle—we were out there having fun, completing the tasks together.

When we finished, I felt so proud, and I was thankful for Pepsi's trust in me and our partnership. She overcame her fears because she felt how much I wanted to ride the trail. Supporting my self-confidence has been one of her biggest gifts to me.

During the years we spent together, Pepsi and I grew very close. She changed from a horse thinking twice about whether to be caught and allow that human to ride her, and became a horse walking toward me, happy to see me, telling the other horses that I am her human.

She became braver, more relaxed, and seemed to be more herself—much like me. Where she had shied away from scary things earlier, she would now walk up to them and take a look at them, maybe even touch them. Instead of being cranky toward other horses around the grooming area, she would stand relaxed and comfortable most times. We came together in a partnership, and it allowed us both to find our own flow.

I know that I would not be where I am without having met and ridden Pepsi. She helped me become more aware of myself, connect to my body and emotions, realize that what happens around me is a reflection of myself, and to open up toward other animals and humans. She made me brave.

I am not sure if I would have been brave enough to leave my old comfortable life in Stuttgart and go on the journey to find myself without everything she taught me. Quitting my secure job and deciding to take up training to become an Animal Therapist brought me in touch with so many fears. Pepsi has played a huge part of my learning to cope and face my fears, so they don't stop me.

What I learned from her also helps me with my clients; I have had more than one situation in which I sensed that the behavior the horse or dog showed was a reflection of myself, the owner, or the environment—and that meant I could solve it.

Thank you, Pepsi, for being my friend and my *spiegel*—mirroring my soul.

About Antonia Feldkamp

———

Antonia is an Animal Therapist from Germany, currently training in Traditional Chinese Veterinary Medicine. She has been passionate about animals, especially horses, her whole life. Antonia loves learning new things with and from horses. She has worked with them in many different ways, from dressage to liberty work, and recently got into horseback archery. What she loves most is to stroll around in nature on horseback and to feel the connection to her inner self deepening due to the soft but strong nature of her horse partner.

Antonia and her partner commute between Canada and Germany but spend most of their time in New Brunswick, Canada.

Dedication

This story is dedicated to every horse and human friend who has guided me on my way and still does. Above all, to Pepsi, who is as much part of this book as I am, her owner Karin, my partner Steve, and my family.

BOOK RECOMMENDATIONS

HorseSpeak: The Equine-Human Translation Guide by Sharon Willie & Gretchen Vogel
Natural Horse-Man-Ship by Pat Parelli
Women Who Run With the Wolves by Clarissa Pinkola Estés, Ph. D

CHAPTER 8

FOLLOWING THE FEEL

BY MINDY SCHNEIDER

———

FOR ME, HORSES are dreams and infinite possibilities. They represent the qualities I hold dear: true beauty, unconditional love, authenticity, freedom, and expression. My life's journey alongside horses has all these qualities and so much more. On this path, I have had many opportunities to learn and grow. Horses have helped raise me and have guided me back home to myself. I would not be the person I am today without their teachings and guidance.

I believe that we are all born dreamers.

Horses came into my life through my daydreams. As a young child, I fell in love with horses as I sat on my grandmother's living room floor watching *Black Beauty*. Anna Sewell appealed to my empathic, highly sensitive, and intuitive soul when she eloquently depicted the heart of the horse. Tears fell from my eyes when Beauty was mistreated. I connected to the fact that Beauty had a deep, rich inner life and was often misunderstood. Deeper layers existed in me, too. Little did I know at the time, I would one day have a Beauty of my own.

From that moment forward, I never shut up about horses, much to the disappointment of my non-horsey family and friends. At age eleven, my aunt and I started taking riding lessons together. Fortunately, she had a love of horses too.

Those early days were filled with trail riding and summer camps. My mother used her sewing skills to make a cape for my lesson horse, which he wore proudly during a Halloween play day. Just kidding... We could not keep it on him. My dad even assisted when I naively signed up to muck a badly matted-down cow pen to work off some lessons. My parents were not horse people, but they saw the spark in me and nurtured my passion.

It did not take long for me to decide I needed an equine partner to call my very own. I made a deal with my mom that I could own one if I studied all things horses for one full year. Through a work connection my mom had, we came to know of a paint horse for sale. He fit the description of what I was looking for perfectly.

At the time, Kona was giving a young girl riding lessons. The family that owned him was into English riding. His owner had formed a close bond with him—how could you not with this gentle, kind horse? Even so she was not interested in Western riding so felt it best to find Kona a suitable home.

I walked into a beautiful barn with cobblestone floors and an attached indoor riding arena, turned to a stall on my right, and there he stood. A proud, beautiful, stockily-built chestnut-and-white paint horse. Straight out of my dreams. My riding instructor at the time came along to test ride Kona. She saddled up and rode along the fence line. Her remarks after the ride were, "This is going to be too much horse for her."

Maybe he was a bit forward for a beginner rider, but this was my horse. The heart wants what the heart wants.

I began self-care boarding at a small, private farm within a five-minute drive of my home. I fed and cared for Kona twice a day. I learned about responsibility and hard work. I vividly remember one lesson on humility that Kona taught me. I have a permanent scar on my right hand in case I ever forget.

While practicing for an upcoming speed show, I was riding in the top pasture where there were poles set for pole bending. I was galloping excessively fast and was headed straight toward the fence. Kona veered left when he approached it, and as I fell off to the right, I grabbed onto the fence.

My hand was bloody and mangled. My feeling afterward was one of guilt, wondering why I was going so fast. Kona always taught me lessons like that when I was too prideful and needed them the most.

Kona has the biggest heart. Almost all of my family, college friends, and ex-boyfriends have been on his back, and he carried them around in the gentlest manner. And he loves kids. When you see him in the pasture, his essence is wisdom and gentle strength. His forwardness and heart really came in handy when we competed at speed shows together.

Kona was born in Arizona and had past experience in reining, roping, and speed events like barrel racing and pole bending. I borrowed an old saddle from my barn owner, and we hauled to shows. I met some wonderful people and formed friendships along the way. My friend Britt rode a tri-colored paint. We would place first or second in each class. It was a challenge to see who would be the champion at the end of the day. I loved flying with my heart horse. There were times we would get into the flow, sync up together, and become one mind and body.

When you are a horse-crazy teen, you join 4-H to be around other horse-crazy teens. I chose the Southern Saddles 4-H Club. I met some great mentors and gained many friends. On the day before a 4-H roundup show, I could not make it out to the barn to get Kona ready. Kelsey, a fellow 4-H club member and friend came to my barn to clip and bathe Kona, so he was ready for me to show the next day. Those were the kind of people I met. Kelsey is now my veterinarian. The year I graduated college, she gifted me with my horse's spring vaccines. Kona is now in his senior years, and when it is time to lay him to rest, it is comforting to know she will be the one to do it.

What I learned during my time in 4-H has proven invaluable. I had the opportunity to hold leadership positions, travel to cool places like the Kentucky Horse Park and participate in competitions. My parents would religiously drive me to hippology, horse bowl, and horse judging practices each week.

Hippology is the study of the horse. It is an individual and team equine knowledge contest. My mentor Deb was a fantastic teacher and experienced horsewoman. She shared her knowledge and passion with all her students. I learned the value of education, how to be a part of a team, and do my part; I gained so much equine knowledge.

Throughout my journey, I have had some great and some not-so-great mentors. Same as with my horses, each mentor showed up right on time. I gained wisdom. I learned how to navigate the horse world and the real world using my intuition. If something felt wrong in my gut, I learned to trust that intuitive knowing. Maya Angelou said, "Do the best you can until you know better. Then when you know better, do better." I find that quote to be true of my horsemanship journey.

I started to get involved in a riding discipline called western pleasure. I had dreams of competing in all-around events at big shows like Quarter Horse Congress and Paint Horse World Show. I started out by taking lessons on Kona. As my skills progressed, I started searching for a show horse that was trained in Western pleasure, one with a little more flair. The prices on some of the horses were astronomical. The search went on for about two years. I requested many videos of horses from all over the states, traveled to test ride some, but none of them felt right.

I was searching on DreamHorse.com late one night and came across an ad for a three-year-old double registered American Quarter Horse/American Paint Horse. Kash was breathtaking. He had a bold, wide, white blaze on his head and three white stockings. I remember seeing this horse and getting that intuitive hit again.

Ah yes, there you are, I have been looking for you.

There were more practical horses I was looking at; Kash was a young, green, three-year-old after all. But when I received the video of him being ridden, I watched it repeatedly.

There was that feeling again—the recognition and knowing. So, I followed the feeling. The next thing I knew, my mom, my trainer, and I were on the road to Georgia with a trailer in tow. The trip was fourteen hours both ways. I first met Kash in a brick barn where he spent a large portion of the day. That was the standard. Most show horses spent their time in stalls with little herd interaction. They would get some individual turnout and were worked in an arena when it was time to exercise or show.

Kash was trailered to an indoor arena so we could see him walk, jog and lope, and then we came back to sign the papers and made it official. I was a horse owner for the second time.

On the trip home, thoughts danced in my head of an announcer's voice saying, "And in first place, it's Mindy Schneider riding On Sudden Impulse!" The dreams and visions I had of placing at those big fancy shows came flooding in. Sometimes dreams lead us to places we could not have even imagined otherwise. To something even greater.

Kash came back to my trainer's barn and entered her training program. His life wasn't much different there than it had been at his previous owner's place. He spent his days hanging out in a stall and working in an arena daily.

I sensed a growing sadness in him, but I had to listen more closely to make sense of the message he was sending. At that point in my horsemanship journey, I thought some of these practices were normal and that every other trainer who trained show horses practiced the same ones. That this was normal life for a show horse.

I kept trying to feel what Kash was telling me and some things started to come to the surface. I arrived for a lesson to see that Kash was in the riding arena. He looked very uncomfortable with one rein tied tightly to the saddle horn, so his neck was sharply bent to one side. He was wearing a western bit with a large port and long shanks. He kept going in small, tight circles to get relief from the pressure. He had angered the trainer, and this was her way to teach him a lesson.

I went another time to the barn and inquired about why the inside of his gaskin muscles looked wrinkled and abnormal. I learned that they had put Palmolive dish soap on this area and it had essentially burned his skin in an attempt to get him to jog slower with his back legs. What? I'd thought this horse had a great jog. His sire was a reserve world champion in western pleasure known for his beautiful, flat-kneed jog.

The show horse world started to look a lot less fancy, shiny, and appealing and more demoralizing, abusive, and depressing. *Is this what my horse must endure daily to do a short trip around a show ring? Is this really my dream? What is my horse's dream?* I wondered on that awhile.

My intuition was yelling at me to get my horse out of this situation. I decided to move both of my horses to another private barn close by with a larger outdoor sand riding ring and a convenient wash stall. Jim, the new barn owner, hitched up his truck and trailer and we drove to pick up Kash.

When he was loaded into the trailer, I felt a sigh of relief. I am not sure if that feeling was my horse's or mine. I have never looked back. It is a tough lesson to learn, but I believe Kash and I had to go through that trial together for a reason.

I decided to train Kash on my own with the help of clinics and expos to explore new ways of training. The first few rides on Kash were explosive and dangerous. I remember getting a clear view of the sky when he reared up. Holes in his training became obvious. He was either reactive, or he shut down. Horses shut down when they don't get a release from pressure; their shutdown becomes a form of learned helplessness. Kash had learned that humans were not to be trusted. The tiniest bit of pressure could be a threat to his survival.

Oftentimes our horses are a mirror of us. I understood Kash's behavior because growing up, I had formed my own protective layers. Emotions ran high and spewed out into my childhood home, creating a chaotic environment with a level of unpredictability. There was an emotional enmeshment where I consciously or unconsciously took on my family member's emotions.

I rarely communicated my needs and instead catered to others' needs, creating codependent patterns. I learned that relationships could be chaotic places full of tough love, similar to the chaos and pressure that Kash experienced in relationships with humans. The level of emotional regulation, emotional intelligence, and unconditional love horses display helped me through a challenging childhood. Accountability and boundaries were also vital lessons learned.

Kash and I competed in 4-H and local shows. We competed in showmanship, western pleasure, western horsemanship, trail, and even dabbled lightly in English riding. We both enjoyed and excelled in the pattern classes like horsemanship and trail. I have totes full of ribbons, plaques, and belt buckles from our show days. More importantly, I have the memories that will last a lifetime—the good ones, along with the learning opportunities.

After a long day of showing, Kash would often be reluctant to load on the trailer. I'd have to get help from others to get him loaded. It would be frustrating when everyone was tired from the day. I remember the day Kash was tied to the trailer and a flock of geese flew over the trailer. Kash pulled back, broke free, and ran around the showgrounds with his tail in the air like an Arabian while performing the floatiest trot. After his "show of one," he was corralled. The award for most embarrassed went to me.

After placing well enough in the county and district shows, we had earned our place in the four-year-old western futurity class. It was a high honor to represent our county at the State show, so anticipation built before the show. We arrived at the expo hall, settled in, and I schooled Kash in the outdoor arena. I slept in the stall next to Kash with the bright expo lights on and the horses munching on hay all night. But that didn't matter. I was next to my horse.

Kash and I entered the ring for our class the next day. It was a large class of about fifteen riders in the indoor arena. We had never competed in an indoor arena before. The stands were right at the horses' eye level as the horses went around. To make matters worse, there were adults with plastic bags and children with peacock feathers. It was frazzling enough for me, and I felt Kash's every muscle tense up underneath me. After a couple of times around the ring, I knew it was best to come into the middle to retire before either of us got hurt.

We were feeding off each other's nerves in that moment. Disaster was averted.

I took the opportunity to practice in more indoor arenas after that hiccup. I was glad my horse kept me safe and that I made the quick decision to honor and respect our fear. I've learned that sometimes we can get injured if we push past what our horse or ourselves are uncomfortable with or nervous about. Even though I was disappointed and embarrassed, it was a great learning opportunity. My horse was looking to me for reassurance. Even though I looked fine, on the inside I was a ball of nerves and in no shape to be leading him. Horses really do know the emotions we try to mask.

Over time, with many trials and errors, Kash and I built a beautiful relationship. The small moments led to the most significant breakthroughs. Once we learned what to focus on, things started to flow. I gradually learned how to speak a horse's language from talented natural horsemanship clinicians and trainers.

I practiced groundwork with Kash, which involved looking for non-verbal cues and gaining his focus and connection from the ground first. Starting on the ground made all the difference since he was hesitant, tense, and nervous when I was in the saddle. I had originally been taught to only lunge the horse to tire him out before climbing in the saddle, so groundwork was a new concept to me. Using these new techniques and with a new mindset, my confidence grew alongside Kash's.

Natural horsemanship felt so right. I could not get enough. I would be on the edge of my seat watching clinicians at expos. Clinicians like Pat Parelli, John Lyons, Guy McLean, Patrick King, and Brendan Wise, to name a few. I was in awe of the way they worked in harmony with their horses without dominance. There was no pain or fear in the horse. There was ease in two-way communication.

This is what I had been missing. The relational way of horsemanship centered on building and maintaining a connection, above all else. Harsh training techniques and tools are not necessary when you truly understand your horse and he understands you back.

The more I worked on the relationship and connection with both of my horses and communicated in a way they understood, the more they blossomed. A brand-new world opened, and I was able to see their rich inner lives—in the arena and in the pasture.

I started more natural horse-keeping methods of 24/7 turnout, barefoot, often bridleless, as well as positive reinforcement and clicker training. Kona and Kash were allowed to have a "voice" and express themselves. Sure, there were times where I wasn't perfect, I lost my temper and acted out, but they always forgave me and saw me for who I was deeper down. Their unconditional love was a guiding light and is a quality that exists in me and all of us.

I got to see this unconditional love on display when I volunteered at a local therapeutic riding program for my high school graduation project. Witnessing the power of horses to heal was an illuminating experience. I also saw how these special animals brought people together. One rider who was unable to move unassisted would sit up tall, laugh, and have a big smile on his face when his horse picked up a trot. A volunteer there learned sign language to be able to communicate with deaf riders. The short time I spent at Normandy Farms had a huge impact on me. Deeply inspired by the horses and volunteers,

I poured my heart into my graduation project and brought Kash to my school as show and tell.

I followed hoofprints through college, studying Animal Science at Delaware Valley University. My college experience was unique in that I received a lot of hands-on instruction during lab classes. My favorite classes were Equine Behavior, Stable Management, and Animal-Assisted Therapies.

I trained a horse named Colten to perform the Spanish walk during my Equine Behavior course. I learned to give injections to the gentle Standardbred broodmares and even showed a broodmare in hand during our college Activities "A-Day" Day horse show.

The most incredible experience was getting to practice and perform gymnastics on horseback. During my time at Delaware Valley University, I joined the Equestrian Vaulting Club. I formed some great friendships in this club. We practiced individual and team maneuvers on a practice barrel and held performance showcases. It took balance and agility to learn the basic and freestyle maneuvers. I even had the opportunity to stand on the back of a horse moving at a canter. The woman who instructed us went on to compete at the World Equestrian Games in Tyron.

Life can be so full of shadow, light, and mystery.

Special people come into our lives to help rekindle our inner spirit, even if only for a season. At the time, I was post-college, and it was tough being back home and away from friendships I had formed during those years.

In December of 2015, Matthew came into my life. Our common connection was our mothers, who worked together and introduced us. Matthew had a bright spirit which showed through his deep brown eyes. He was forever lighthearted, childlike, and jovial. You could always find him dancing, making jokes, and loving his family, especially his twin sister, aunt, and niece. He introduced me to the Grateful Dead and music festivals, which are still my favorite. He took the most beautiful sunset photographs, and we talked about backpacking trips we'd take one day.

Even the brightest sun will eventually turn into the darkest moon. I remember getting the call on that day in August of 2016.

"They found a white truck, and they think it's his," the caller said.

I fell to my knees. My heart sank. I knew he was gone. I pounded the floor in anger.

"How could you do this to me, to your family?" I cried out.

Matthew slipped away at the age of thirty-one from an accidental drug overdose. He made his transition and left behind grieving friends and family.

My horses were there to hold space and lift me up as my heart was full of heaviness. My grieving process involved them.

Matthew is now a part of the ether. This I know is true. He guides us from beyond and sends us signs that he is still around, if only in spirit. I am re-attached to the great mystery of life. The light shines again in the darkness.

While Matthew was still earthside, I saw a video for a local women's addiction recovery farm. I sent it to him and said, "I am going to be a part of this organization."

"You're going to change people," he responded.

Grief is the price we pay for love. As I grieved with Matthew's family, I knew we needed an outlet. We went to one of the meetings for the Char Hope Foundation together and we have been volunteering there ever since.

The Char Hope Foundation is a sober-living farm in Pylesville, Maryland, that helps women recover from addiction using agricultural-based practices. I lead the equine program, where I help to train the horses that come into the program and develop the resident's horsemanship skills. I also lead workshops with outside recovery groups that come to the farm for equine-assisted learning and interaction.

The horse's honest, in-the-moment feedback helps me to guide the individual or group to breakthrough moments during a session or workshop. The residents and participants co-regulate with the horses, develop a transformative bond, and open up during the interactions. It is very effective. Through the partnership with horses, humans heal, overcome trauma, deepen spiritual principles, and become empowered.

In October 2020, Char Hope acquired a beautiful buckskin mare named Cheyenne for their program. Little was known about her history since she came from an auction. We figured it wasn't all that pretty judging from her behavior. She would plow through people to get out of her stall, walk in front of a person when she was being led, and you could often see fear when the whites of her eyes showed.

I knew this mare was in flight or freeze mode and that she perceived any pressure as a threat. I instinctively knew she needed time to unwind, rewire, and above all, she needed a partner to bond with. Using what I have learned with Kash, I helped guide Olivia—the Char Hope Farm Manager—and Cheyenne to form a partnership. Olivia started as a beginner rider and has developed deeper empathy, self-awareness, and a positive mindset that benefited her life and career. They are now both relaxed, confident, and trusting.

I have benefited from equine therapy my whole life. It has been an extraordinary blessing to spend my life in the presence of these wise creatures and let them guide me home. I wanted to share the transformational experience of forming an equine partnership with others. It truly lights me up to share this passion by facilitating workshops and teaching riding lessons. I feel it is my soul's mission.

So, I followed the feeling. I have recently launched an equine-assisted coaching business. My clients will get the opportunity to do the work and grow alongside horses to enhance their personal development, mindset, spirituality, leadership, and meet their goals.

Horses continue to fuel my dreams. It only makes sense they are right next to me as I step into this next chapter and I am bringing others along on this wild, enlightening ride.

About Mindy Schneider

Mindy is based in Maryland and has spent seventeen years learning from and growing with horses. She partners with her two horses to guide people to practice self-awareness and mindfulness, overcome obstacles, and reconnect with their authentic selves as an Equine Guided Coach. She also facilitates equine experience workshops for men and women in addiction recovery. Mindy's horsemanship journey has been an evolution. She started in 4-H and FFA, competing in western riding, hippology, horse bowl, and horse judging. She has hot-walked Thoroughbred racehorses, driven draft horses, volunteered in hippotherapy, and performed in equestrian vaulting.

Mindy has a bachelor's degree in Animal Science and is a lifelong learner and seeker. Her intention in sharing her story is to empower other equestrians and non-horse people alike to follow their hearts and intuition and fully enjoy the journey.

Dedication

To my family, friends, mentors, and my love, who support my dreams. To my equine partners for their wisdom and unconditional love.

BOOK RECOMMENDATIONS

The Horse Boy: A Father's Quest to Heal His Son by Rupert Issacson
Women Who Run With the Wolves by Clarissa Pinkola Estés, Ph.D.
The Body Keeps The Score by Bessel Van Der Kolk, M.D.

CHAPTER 9

ASK YOURSELF

BY STEFANIE LY

"Right now you are being herded into a situation. You may not know how you came to be here. There are barriers ahead; however, they may be only an illusion. You have been going along with the herd, but it may be time for you to rethink your strategy and your personal plan. If you have arrived at this juncture without a sense of knowing how you got there, look at those around you. Ascertain if the company you are in now is the company you wish to continue with on the journey, or is it time to seek a new direction. Ask yourself what standards and what direction will take you to the perfect destination in your future. Reflect, look about, and make a conscious choice to belong or move apart."
Touched by a Horse Inspirational Cards - Melisa Pearce

I BEGIN EACH MORNING by pulling a card from one of the oracle decks I have collected over the years. I reflect on the words and I journal, a self-care habit I witnessed my mother practice for as long as I can remember. *Touched by a Horse: Whispers From A Horse's Heart Inspirational Cards* is my new favorite deck.[1] This deck was created by Melisa Pearce, teacher, author, psychotherapist, and pioneer in the field of human / horse healing. Jan Taylor's bold use of colors and brushstrokes brought life and emotion through the images on the cards. I love the way that the messages in these cards are always exactly what I need to hear.

When I pulled that particular card for my daily ritual of reflective journaling, I wasn't sure what to make of it. When I first read the words on the card, I let myself be open to consider what was arising in my consciousness from its wisdom. What was it that my guides wanted me to know? Would this card really inspire an answer to the questions I was holding concerning my future?

I read the card once more, picking out the parts that ignited something in me, and wrote in my journal. I asked myself what standards and what direction would take me to the perfect destination in my future. I reflected, looked about, and made a conscious choice to belong or move apart.

Four years ago, when I began the journey I am on now, I had just transitioned out of an eleven-year marriage. The final years of my marriage were full of the challenges that provided ample opportunity for couples to grow together or deepen the divide. For us, the crack in the foundation had grew larger by the year. Eventually, the whole house came crashing down.

I was experiencing physical and emotional pain. I sought support from doctors and specialists to no avail. Migraines, panic attacks, vertigo, asthma, neuralgia, and swelling in my extremities. No one could find a cause, which only increased my sense of despair.

What was my body trying to tell me? When no diagnosis or acute illness could be identified, I decided it was time to go to therapy.

On the outside, I looked as though I had it all together, like icing that covers a crumbling cake; it was just a show. What people could not see was that I was falling apart. I was great at convincing the world I was great despite the daily struggle of living with acute anxiety.

After reading Gabor Mate's famous book *When the Body Says No: The Hidden Cost of Stress*,[2] I was finally able to consider that all of my detachment, dissociation, and pushing down of emotions as I hid that I was suffering might be what was making this physical and mental assault on my body louder and louder.

I found a somatic-based therapist, someone who takes a "holistic therapeutic approach, and incorporates the body, mind, spirit, and emotions in the healing process."[3] Finally, I decided to let whatever needed to come to the surface be said out loud to a receptive listener and so be released.

Through this therapeutic relationship, I began to listen to what years of denying my own needs and quieting my own voice were trying to tell me. My mind and body had given up. I had subconsciously decided that I needed out, and if I was not going to take action, my body would do it for me.

I worked in a hospital at the time and had witnessed what it looks like when someone's subconscious mind makes this decision. The feeling was palpable. While my mind thought maybe everyone would be better without me, my heart knew that my children needed me. My work here was not done. I decided I needed to use every ounce of my being to step forward in a different direction.

Starting that journey felt terrifying. I slid into a deep depression, on the brink of suicide, telling no one how bad things had become. In a synchronistic way, I was invited to participate in a self-development leadership course through a volunteer role I held at my children's school that spring.

I decided to enroll with the support of my best friend of thirty years, who was willing to take the course with me, so I didn't have to experience the overwhelming social anxiety of a room full of strangers on my own. Throughout the course, I had many breakdowns and breakthroughs. Through the process, I was able to reconnect with myself, and let go of so many of the stories of the past that I had held on to as limiting beliefs for why life hadn't worked out the way I thought it should have.

I learned that leaders allow themselves to feel and be vulnerable. The leaders there demonstrated this, which gave others permission to do so.

I had undergone an emotional and spiritual transformation, and the result was accepting the choice to separate from my husband, even though I knew that the years ahead would be challenging, and I did not want to tear apart my family.

After making this decision, I began the journey back to wellness for the first time in years. I was consciously willing to take responsibility and create the life I was here to live. I would no longer allow anyone, or the self-inflicted barriers in my mind, to stand in the way.

With this renewed clarity, reconnection to my voice, and the distinction of being at the cause of my life, not at the effect of it, I stepped forward into this next phase. I was committed to three things: grounded, heart-led leadership; supporting the wellbeing of families and children, including my own; and resuming a journey I had started years before: being with horses.

I wanted to find a way to connect these things but had no idea how to do so. Beyond reason and having no clue how to draw the connection between those three pillars, one thing I knew for sure was that I needed to find a way to be around horse energy as much as possible.

Though I have loved and had opportunities to spend time with horses here and there throughout my life, my understanding was that family finances kept me away from the barn in the typical lessons and Pony Club. My first experience with a horse was right around my parents' divorce when I was five years old.

My aunt owned a mare named Margie, and she was boarded at a stable, just down the street from my house. My dad's new partner had a love of horses and had been an avid equestrian since she was a child. My dad knew that I loved animals and thought a farm would be the perfect place to introduce me to her. We spent some time together at the farm. My aunt allowed me to ride Margie, who was a gentle, kind soul and was described as "wonderful when I rode her." Margie was only with us for six months, as an episode of colic ended her life suddenly. My aunt was able to find another horse; however, she and her husband moved to Nova Scotia not long after, and that was the end of my time at the barn.

I believe in my body and soul that this memory and this experience, and the connection with this horse at this tender age and vulnerable time of my life has never left me. It was an acute feeling I have longed to recreate.

The leadership course created such a shift in my energy and ground of being that my insides and outsides finally aligned. After, I demonstrated authentic confidence in my life and my volunteer role at my children's school in particular. When the opportunity for the position of School Administrator presented itself the following year, I jumped at the chance and applied. After navigating a series of progressively challenging interviews, I was awarded the position! I couldn't have been happier. One area of my life aligned with my vision: serving children and families as a servant leader in an incredible school community.

This opportunity was sweetened by the ability to be close and available to my daughter daily, an experience that I had not foreseen as exceptional until the separation. With this aspect of my life falling into place, I moved forward into the next—being with horses.

I am a self-identified lifelong learner, passionate about research, the pursuit of knowledge, and I love to read. My friends joke that you cannot look around a room in my house without seeing a pile of books on a surface. I naturally spent my free time searching the Internet for opportunities to be with and work with horses, hoping one would stand out and speak to my heart.

My research of "how" created visions of jumping the fence and riding bareback into the woods—a true novice fantasy indeed, likely fueled by childhood movies! Between daydreams, I found a variety of equine education courses at universities and private businesses as a starting point. Though there were a number of programs available, nothing felt quite right, and most programs required personal access to horses and a background of equestrian skills and years of experience, neither of which I had. I then began to consider applying for entry-level jobs in the equine industry.

I quickly discovered that I would need way more experience even for the most basic of positions, but this time, I moved through that circumstantial barrier quickly, kept an open mind, and I just kept searching. I had faith that somewhere, somehow, there would be an opportunity that would be perfect for me. Then, all of a sudden, it happened. I came across a short equine behavior course at a local university with a reputation for excellence in the equine world.

At the same time, I came across a volunteer opportunity through their website at a therapeutic riding barn not too far from home that only required a willingness to learn, punctuality, and commitment—not horse expertise—to get started!

Thankful that I had not given up too soon and that I had some flexibility in my work schedule due to evening meetings, I jumped at the chance, quickly applied, and was accepted into their training program. Just days after seeing the advertisement, I was learning all about grooming and tack and leading a beautiful Passafina mare named Tempi.

With the education and the opportunity to develop experience falling into place, I set off on the path with joy and hope in my heart. I realized that the barriers to what we genuinely want often look like our expectations and our old limiting beliefs—what we think it should look like. We turn a blind eye to the possibility that it could look different and still be amazing. We give up all too easily. With this willingness to just get started, I began my journey—one small step at a time.

At the therapeutic riding barn, I was blessed to be partnered with a well-experienced volunteer. She was retired from her career and now volunteered at the barn full time. She shared with me that she felt the call to horses after her husband passed away, even though she didn't have a lot of experience beforehand. At that point, she couldn't imagine her life without them. She was a straight-talking kind of woman. She would tell you exactly how it was; if you were doing something that wasn't right—you'd soon know it.

As much as this type of personality can rub some people the wrong way, I loved it. I've come to terms with my people-pleasing ways, not saying how I feel as a way of controlling how I'm seen or trying to manage other people's feelings. I have learned that this pattern of behavior keeps me small and stuck, not asking for what I need, not setting boundaries, and not being fully who I am being called to be.

In this experience, as a novice horse person, I didn't need someone to ignore my mistakes and help me feel good. I needed someone to train me to be a capable and safe lead walker because I was responsible for an arena full of children and horses. My mentor shared that she appreciated my willingness to learn from her and that I accepted her feedback graciously. I imagined how her previous experiences may not have always worked out that way. In my younger years, I might also have shied away and interpreted her directness as an attack, most likely her words to mean that I was unsuitable for working with horses, and I should forget about it.

I appreciated the freedom that my path had created. I was able to take in the information and release the judgment, allowing the feedback to transform my abilities and increase my confidence. After a few weeks together, we became close through the colder winter weather and shared more about our lives as we groomed and tacked up our horses and led the students around the arena for their exercises. She would often comment on how natural, calm, and supportive I was with the students from a special education program at a local school.

It wasn't always easy for them to feel safe and comfortable on such a large animal. Our energy as lead and side walkers supported their experience and put them at ease. It was an experience I won't soon forget. I know the skills Tempi and my volunteer mentor taught me are the very foundation on which the rest of my experiences have been built. It was empowering for me and, as a result, the children we supported during their lessons were also empowered. Mission accomplished, or so I thought.

Much to my dismay, I was only able to participate for one season as a volunteer because the winter weather prevented me from committing to a forty-five-minute drive down poorly cleared country roads. I was registered and looking forward to being back at the barn for the spring term. Then COVID-19 hit, and well, the world shut down, including all horse barns, schools, and riding programs.

Disappointed, I wondered what this would mean for me. When would I have the next opportunity to be back at the barn? How would I be able to deepen my experience with horses? What was the path ahead?

As a way to help horse people stay connected during the lockdown, the University of Guelph offered a free course through their Equine Guelph program: Equine Sickness Prevention. I decided to enroll, feeling at the time that this was the best bet to stay on my path. Diving into the realm of equine illness helped build knowledge and helped to further contextualize our government's decisions about quarantine during a time of a highly transmissible virus, as this is a normal process for certain equine illnesses too.

Aside from work and the equine course, I was in my eighth round of coaching for the leadership development workshop I had attended, the one that began this journey. I was committed to staying in the conversation that has saved my life in the service of others. That too had to pivot online, which opened up the possibility that it could expand outside of our local community and allow people from all over the world to register!

The course I was coaching this time around was about communication. How our words hold power, and how they hold possibility. While coaching this course in May of 2020, my mindset began to slip. The feeling of being overwhelmed started to set in.

I was frustrated with so many things: with the inability to be close to horses due to the shutdown world that was beyond my control; and holding a lot of responsibility with my job; supporting my children through the lockdown and having their whole worlds turned upside down; only attending school and talking to friends through screens: and then there was coaching. I felt out of balance.

I was reminded that if being with horses was something I really wanted, I needed to create a specific declaration about it. The problem was, I was not just overwhelmed by the fact that I was missing horses, but also that I did not know how exactly I wanted to be and work with them.

I came across a podcast that featured Gabrielle Berstein, an American author considered to be a "next-generation thought leader," and found that her work is also informed by a text I had been working through the summer prior, at the start of my separation, *A Course in Miracles*.[4] I was quickly motivated to read her newest book *Super Attractor: Methods for Manifesting a Life Beyond Your Wildest Dreams*.[5]

One day, feeling at a particular standstill, yet being willing to look inward instead of sitting there in frustration, I completed a meditation and held this question in mind: What is my path? As I did this, I asked for a sign, as Gabrielle suggests.

The sign came to me as a white horse. At the time, I journaled about it, then started to research again about careers that involve horses since I relished my time with the volunteer program. Still, I felt something was missing. Was there was something more I could do to support these children that would also be enjoyable for the horses, where children could collaborate with them as true partners.

Then, I saw it. There was a social media video of a woman I had started following years before. Someone at a store I frequent had visited her farm a few years prior. I looked her up, liked her page, and then forgot about it. I didn't realize Mena Canonico at Liberty Lane was a Facilitator of Equine Experiential Learning (FEEL) and in her video, she was sharing a card with an image of a white horse on it!

The message read: "Go Within. To walk alone right now is part of your journey. Trust your own inner knowingness to guide you through this passage. This is your own walk. This is your personal journey and your destination must remain open and unknown to you at this time. Take the time to look within. Do not run or rush, nor create distraction. You are being asked to steadily walk, breathing in deeply and fully, finding your way a solitary step at a time. Each step takes you further into the unknown for now. Trust that you will be protected and shown the way from deep within. Be strong and do not spook easily. You are surrounded by more protection than you are aware of. Take each step away from the chaos and your usual means of support, to go quietly within. Only then will the lesson reveal itself so you can rejoin the herd."[6]

Wow. That message. And with that, it's what I did. I let it all go to the universe and gave myself the space I needed while knowing that somehow, someday, I would need to reach out and start a conversation with this woman like the universe was asking me to.

Days later, an exercise came up in the communication course that asked the participants to create an alter ego. We were to create someone who has the skills, the energy, the drive, the experience we want—yet is a stretch from our "everyday selves" as we know them and then we had to embody this alternate identity for a class.

It was then that I decided I would embody a strong businesswoman who owned a ranch and was surrounded by family and horses. She had a long table for all of the families she would welcome to family retreats; the people who were struggling to hear and see one another and needed the space and support to reconnect with themselves and each other. She had the energy and passion of two women who I find inspiring, though neither are famous horsewomen: Reese Witherspoon and Joanna Gaines. I researched them both, recorded quotes that inspired me, watched videos about their lives and the things that matter to them, and then created my own version.

With this alter ego, "Reese Gaines," dressed in a white lace shift dress, denim jacket, cowboy hat, and boots, I spoke confidently about the life I wanted to create as if it were the life I was living. With the energy of this experience, I created a vision board, quickly pulling from a huge pile of magazines every image that spoke to the energy of that vision, no matter what it was.

With that, the energy started to move. I came across something I had not heard of before, the terms Equine Assisted Learning and Equine Facilitated Learning. After a bit more research, I learned that these modalities of working with horses as sentient partners and guides transform people's lives and that idea resonated in my heart.

After lamenting that "one day when I have horses, I can do this," I discovered that was just another limiting belief. I didn't actually need my own horses to do this work! I could lease horses to work with from someone else. I breathed a sigh of relief as a huge barrier came crashing down.

I began to investigate programs and quickly realized that none of the programs available were running locally because of COVID-19. Many of these programs appeared to be oriented more toward a business model that didn't resonate: a week-long course, and then off you go!

Again, I let the idea go, I mean, I had never actually experienced a session myself, so maybe the limitations set forth by the hold in programming was the universe's way of redirection. I kept working my day job and focusing on the leadership coaching program.

In June, during a weekend course I was coaching with graduates from the program, I supported participants in creating their next action steps for their lives beyond their limiting beliefs and current circumstances. During a lunch break, as many do, I was drawn to scroll through social media, and I saw a post from Mena, the woman who shared the card with the image of the white horse. The restrictions were lifting, and she was planning a small outdoor gathering on the Solstice Wisdom Circle with the Freedom Herd. I decided to take a leap and register, despite circumstances of limited finances and time.

The experience of that day was truly life-changing. The day began in a little room in the barn. The room was cozy and warm, despite the threat of a storm outside. We began a conversation about why we were there that day, a small group of four of us, as well as Mena and her intern, Andie. I shared, boldly and clearly that I was here to have this experience to support a decision I was making around whether or not to pursue the same path I'd been on, for working with people and horses in the same way. Once everyone had stated their intention, we moved on to learn about the distinction between the voice of the ego—our automatic thoughts that are based in survival—and the higher self. Then, at last, it was time to meet the horses.

When the barn doors opened, I saw her right away, a white horse, staring boldly right back at me. My sign again, living and breathing—just a few meters in front of me! I knew at that moment that she had called me to the farm and to this experience. I had not been around horses at liberty in a very long time. I could feel the nerves rise in my body. My ego immediately shouted at me: "How are you going to do this work if you are afraid of horses at liberty?"

Thankfully, Mena supported me in transforming this story and grounding myself. Throughout the experience, I was tuned in to my body, the way it felt, and the stories and thoughts that came up—then I released them. I was supported and experiencing the impact of my energy through the response of this graceful Arabian mare, who I was introduced to as Mia—also my daughter's name!—I could feel, on a soul level, that I was being called to do this work.

In a follow-up call with Mena after the program, I stated my intentions: I wanted to learn more about facilitated equine experiential learning and be in service to her vision of a retreat center.

The very next week, I started a journey of further development as a horsewoman and mentee, caring for and learning from the Freedom Herd: eight horses with varied pasts and that had come together in the service of others. I learned from experience, taking on more involved horse care than I had at the therapeutic riding barn, including feeding, and other typical barn chores, like repairing broken fences. I even helped with an electrical outage that caused the water buckets to freeze over in the winter and helped when there was a fire at the farm across the road!

By the winter, I began taking on a few practice clients for facilitated equine experiences. The response was clear: My clients were moved by their time with the herd and appreciated my warm and gentle approach. It wasn't always easy. There were challenges, both real and imagined. I experienced the end of life for a member of the herd with whom I had bonded over the summer. Other times I struggled thinking there was something wrong when really the issue was just being in my head thinking—*ego!*— instead of being present with the horse I was working with.

Being with horses has supported me through many challenging moments and transitions across my life, from my parents' divorce to my own separation. The following spring, while caring for the herd independently for six weeks, something I could only have dreamed of doing the year before, I experienced the most difficult loss in my life thus far, the death of my beloved grandmother, Nonna.

The past year through the pandemic and rolling lockdowns had been a disruption to our relationship. When I was a child, Nonna had quit her job to take care of my brother and me, and we had remained very close over the years.

Before the pandemic, Nonna and I attended church every weekend, followed by lunch at a restaurant, where we caught up on life, both current and reminiscing about the good old days. She would often share joyfully about her childhood, growing up on a farm in Italy during World War II. I can only imagine what her reality there was like. Although her family was not directly involved in the war, her father was killed in a bombing on his way to deliver lumber one afternoon when she was just thirteen years old. That's my daughter's age now.

It was not an easy childhood, yet, she always told stories about how much she loved having everyone in her large family working, eating, and spending time together on that farm, and how they were always laughing. Not seeing one another was hard for both of us, but the message was loud and clear—staying home protected her.

It was Easter Sunday, and I received a phone call from my mum that I was finally allowed to visit, but Nonna had already slipped into a coma. As I sat at her bedside, holding her hand, on our last Sunday together, I grieved the loss of not only her but everything we were to one another and how her presence was like a light in this world. She was my biggest fan—so proud and confident that I could accomplish anything I put my mind to.

When I left her bedside that evening, I received a response from a scholarship I had applied for to take an intensive equine business course and acknowledged that as the receipt of a gift from the beyond. *Thank you, Nonna—I know you are still looking after me.* The following day I was on my way to the feed store when I got the news of her passing. I drove straight to the barn as the horses were relying on me to feed them.

As I opened the barn door, there they were, the lead mare Anya and gelding, Dream, both lying down, next to one another, a scene which I had never come across until that day or since. Usually, one would stand guard as the other slept or relaxed. Seeing them lying there together was a clear message as if to say that my Nonna had joined my Nonno in the afterlife, after six long years apart.

We are together now; we are safe; we are at peace.

It is moments like these that I have experienced and witnessed during daily chores and equine facilitated experiences alike. Horses have such generous wisdom to share when we are truly present with them.

Through continued courses, reading, from my mentor Mena, and many other horsewomen and men, I have learned so much about horses, their wellbeing, and their capacity for healing. I have stepped out of my comfort zone and beyond the limitations of my ego.

It has been just over a year since I met the Freedom Herd at the Summer Solstice Wisdom Circle, and I have had so many beautiful moments on the farm in the presence of this herd. Some of these moments I have shared with those closest to me, including my daughter. While she is adamant that she is not a "horse girl" she still finds an immediate connection when present with the herd and she loves taking care of them.

I know that I have many more years ahead to continue to develop my skills, people to meet and learn from, and horses to work with. One thing I know for sure, I will stay true to my values and allow the path I am on to unfold with patience, just as my soul intended. I will continue to reflect on the experiences along the way, tune in daily to my higher self, take conscious actions that align with the truth in my heart, and support others to do the same— all in partnership with horses.

References

1. Touched by a Horse. "Meet Melisa Pearce." Accessed July 24, 2021. https://touchedbyahorse.com/meet-melisa-pearce/

2. Maté, Gabor. *When the Body Says No: The Cost of Hidden Stress*. Toronto: Random House, 2004.

3. GoodTherapy. "Somatic Psychotherapy." Accessed July 23, 2021. https://www.goodtherapy.org/learn-about-therapy/types/somatic-psychotherapy

4. Foundation for Inner Peace. *A Course in Miracles: Combined Volume (3 Combined ed.)*. Mill Valley, CA: Foundation for Inner Peace, 2007.

5. Bernstein, Gabriel. *Super Attractor: Methods for Manifesting a Life beyond Your Wildest Dreams*. Carlsbad, CA: Hay House UK LTD, 2019.

6. Touched by a Horse. "Meet Melisa Pearce." Accessed July 24, 2021. https://touchedbyahorse.com/meet-melisa-pearce/

About Stefanie Ly

Stefanie is a Waldorf School Administrator in Ontario, Canada, and is on the path of certification for Equine Facilitated Wellness. Her journey with horses has been one of connection through "being with" and creating relationships on the ground with these majestic, sentient beings. With degrees in Fine Art and Developmental Psychology, her highest goal is to serve children and families by integrating creativity and wellness through therapeutic art and equine facilitated experiences, supporting the development of authentic connection and grounded leadership in homes and at school.

Dedication

This story is dedicated to all those in my life who have provided me with support and presented me with challenges; both elements create opportunities for growth and adventure, enriching our stories and our lives.

Book Recommendations

The Wild in Us by Thirza Voysey
The Compassionate Equestrian: 25 Principles to Live by When Caring and Working with Horses by Allen Schoen and Susan Gordon
Hold on to Your Kids by Dr. Gordon Neufeld
Simplicity Parenting by Kim John Payne

CHAPTER 10
CHASING HOLLYWOOD
BY NADINE SMITH

———

HORSES HAVE BEEN the center of my world for as long as I can remember. As a child, I spent all my before and after school time adoring, caring for, and riding my pony. I worked many long hours at a riding stable as a teenager, which truly was a dream job for a horse-crazy girl. My parents also worked very hard and supported my love of horses, but financially it was up to me to pay for anything they needed. So much of my time was spent working to pay for board and horse care that there wasn't much time or money left over for entering competitions. I never cared that I missed opportunities for sports, other activities, or adventures with friends because horses were my passion in life.

When I was eighteen, I was admiring a beautiful dun Quarter Horse at the barn where I boarded. His owner told me he was trained for something called reining and explained a little about spins and sliding stops. I was intrigued! She talked about his breeding and how he was related to a famous horse called Hollywood Dun It and said that someday reining could be in the Olympics. As it turns out, that was right around the time he was inducted into the NRHA Hall of Fame, and although reining hasn't made it to the Olympics *yet*, there is still hope. The details may be fuzzy, but I'll forever remember that day as the day I set my sights on having my own beautiful Hollywood Dun It reining horse.

Somewhere along the way, as many of us do, I put my passion for horses on the back burner for post-secondary education, furthering my career and building a life with my new husband Mark. An important part of building our life together involved packing up and moving back and forth across Canada as he worked his way through medical school, residency, and establishing a family medicine practice.

For about eight years, I didn't quite feel myself. Something was missing. Deep down, I knew that something was horses. If you have that passion for horses running through your blood, you know the feeling of despair that starts to creep in when you're away from them for too long. The longing for horses is like a dark shadow that comes over you until you put your hand on a horse and you are lit up from the inside again.

Rather than being content with having a small piece of horses in my life, I had an all-or-nothing attitude. I didn't ride, take lessons, learn, train, or even read about horses for years. It just felt too painful. If I couldn't have a horse of my own or a regular opportunity to ride, I thought it would be easier to live life apart from horses until I had more time, space, and could afford a horse of my own again. Then and only then, life would be how it was meant to be, and all the pieces would fall into place.

In hindsight, I see how unnecessary it was to close off from horses altogether during that time. I would have been more advanced in my horsemanship, riding, and maybe could have helped some people through volunteering. As they say, hindsight is 20/20, and that was only the first big lesson I had to learn when it came to mixing a passion for horses and "real life."

In 2014, Mark and I decided to move home to Atlantic Canada to be closer to our families and put down some roots. Knowing we were finally settled in one place and financially ready meant it was time to start the hunt for my dream horse. Before moving from Saskatchewan to Nova Scotia, we went to see an adorable red dun Quarter Horse, Hollywood Jem, that checked all my boxes. Woody, as he was called around the barn, was four years old, had some professional training, was quiet, sweet, and was a great-grandson of *the* Hollywood Dun It! We made arrangements to have him shipped across the country one month after we arrived at our new home.

The day he walked off the trailer was one of the happiest days of my life. His arrival had much more meaning than simply buying a new horse. He was the first horse I had owned as an adult. This horse was the one I searched for and *chose* for the reasons I had been dreaming of for what felt like my entire life. I was going to compete with him; we were going to learn the sport of reining and conquer all kinds of obstacle challenges together. It was finally time for horses to be the center of my world again! It was an amazing and surreal time.

It felt almost as if I had been starved of my passion for so long that I wanted to ride every single day and do *all* the things at once. In our first year together, I learned an incredible amount; we went to many clinics of various disciplines, took lessons, and hauled to our first horse shows. I'm so appreciative of the support of my husband during that first year. He jumped right into being a horse husband, which was a new world for him. Until that summer, he had only heard about my obsession with horses. Living with it was an entirely different beast.

The progress Woody and I made was amazing over the first couple of years. We worked out lots of kinks, and with the help of some professionals, we were doing liberty, could run a reining pattern, and get through an extreme trail course. I wasn't ready for everything I worked on with Woody to be put on hold, but life outside of horses was progressing just as quickly as they were inside life with horses and things were about to change drastically.

In July of 2016, we welcomed our son, Anderson, into our little family. I had stopped riding for the majority of my pregnancy, but I did continue with groundwork and liberty training and spent most of my afternoons with Woody right up until I was ready to deliver. Not long after we brought Anderson home, I started feeling those old feelings of despair and longing for equine therapy again.

As do many parents-to-be, throughout my pregnancy we had talked about how the baby would just come with us wherever we went, sleep when he's tired, and we'd basically just continue on living life as we had been with our additional little bundle of joy. No matter how much you plan, babies have a way of showing you that it's even more important to be adaptable.

I was deeply in love with Anderson from the very beginning. Being a devoted and protective mother was instinctual and immediate. He needed me more than anyone ever had, and he had no problem making that very clear!

At only a few weeks old, it was obvious that our little boy had colic, not the kind of colic I was educated in and that horses get, but the cry-all-day-and-all-night-for-unknown-reasons-kind that babies get. The only relief we got from the crying was if *I* held him.

We tried every recommendation from well-meaning friends and family to no avail—swaddling, rocking, vibrating chairs, car rides, strollers, the list goes on and on. We even tried letting him "cry it out" once, which left me traumatized, and I swore that I'd hold him forever and never sleep again before I'd ever let him cry alone in his room.

Nothing else worked—only my arms. There was no nap time relief either; for eight full months, he either slept with or on me. It was a bittersweet time; so many snuggles and so much love, but also such deep exhaustion, loneliness, and guilt.

It is clear where the exhaustion came from, and I believe most moms feel or experience a level of loneliness as they navigate motherhood for the first time. The guilt also came from what felt like neglecting the horses that were thankfully boarded at a nearby barn. Not only did we have Woody, but we had also bought my husband a unicorn of a mare only five short weeks before I was due.

When Anderson was eight months old, we finally got him sleeping in his room alone, and I moved back into bed with my husband.

Sleep deprivation, exhaustion, post-pregnancy hormones, breastfeeding, major life changes, and isolation are all things that can be hard on a person mentally, physically, and emotionally. Stack all of those factors together, and the recipe for postpartum depression seems obvious. Still, when you're living it, it feels like you're just struggling to maintain normalcy while you're feeling the most tired you've ever been, and are more emotionally heavy than you've ever experienced.

Once in a while, a friend who had a baby only a year and a half before me would ask if I felt like I was through the fog yet. Even though the answer was no, the same answer I gave for over two years, I truly didn't think I had postpartum depression. It wasn't until one day, I was in my car, fighting back the tears, that I drove to my doctor's office and walked in without an appointment to ask if I could see her on the spot.

Having worked in a medical clinic I knew it was worth a try—medical office staff tend to take people who arrive in tears very seriously. Thank goodness for an understanding receptionist who I'm sure has seen many an emotional mother; she put me right into a room. I *still* didn't think I was depressed. I was functioning. I adored my baby. I got through the days just like any other mom, and my husband, who's a family physician, hadn't questioned a thing.

It was when the doctor asked me, "Do you have happy days?"

That took me aback, and that's when it hit me.

"No." I said, full-on crying by then, "I have happy moments, but I don't remember the last time I had a happy day."

Afterward, I got back in the car where I had left my son in the care of my mom, who was completely unaware of what I had gone into the office for, and went on with my day, as usual, mentally preparing to explain to my husband that evening what I had discussed with my doctor.

Most parents can relate to the feelings of exhaustion during the first couple of years of having a child. We all cope in our own ways, and everyone has their struggles. Mine was somewhat self-inflicted, I believe, due to internal pressures, but also somewhat out of my control.

I did not have a typical Canadian maternity leave. I worked for my husband's practice, and people depended on me to continue working, primarily from home. I worked until the day before I gave birth and was answering calls and emails the week after. My job wasn't physically demanding and was maintainable part-time; however, it was still a huge mental stress with a new baby. I remember getting up at 4:30 am to work on accounting tasks because it was the only time I could get out of bed with the best chance of Anderson not waking up immediately.

We also had two dogs, who up until this time were our only babies. I felt a lot of guilt for the attention and exercise they weren't getting. Then there were the horses.

Knowing my horses were getting their basic needs met through their boarding barn did very little to minimize the sadness I was feeling about not spending time with them like I was used to. I had expected a few weeks, maybe a couple of months of downtime for healing and bonding with my new little man, but as the months rolled on with rare trips to the barn feeling rushed and stressful, I became more and more desperate to reconnect with Woody.

The pressure I put on myself to continue to progress in training and to ride consistently only managed to cause frustration and confusion with him. There's no question that my anxiety and rush to get things accomplished resulted in some loss of trust and a lack of his confidence in me as a leader.

The following summer, when Anderson was a year old, I started attending groundwork and riding clinics again, focusing on reining and obstacle challenges. I can pinpoint the day that the cracks in our relationship and trust started to break open. We were taking part in an extreme trail clinic at our boarding barn. It was a sunny but very windy day, and we were riding outside. We had spent hours trail riding and working on trail obstacles over the past couple of years, but for some reason, on that day, he started to refuse obstacles that we had done easily in the past.

One particular obstacle was new, and unfortunately, I didn't realize when we walked up to it that it wasn't a simple walk-over bridge; it was on rolling logs. He put one hoof on it, and as soon as he shifted his weight, it rolled away from him, and he jumped back.

I was equally surprised about the new, frightening obstacle and didn't ask him to approach or attempt to step onto it again. I believe that this moment in time, which evidently was captured in a photo, was the catalyst to the breakdown of our relationship. After that, he refused to stand by a gate that we would open daily. He wouldn't stand on a platform, go through water, and he would no longer go over a teeter-totter comfortably.

These were all things he had done successfully in the past, and in my stressed and exhausted state, I couldn't see that he needed me to slow down and go back to the basics to help him with his confidence again. At that time, I was so hyper-focused on getting to the competitions that I had been waiting for and working toward that I neglected to see that I was responsible for my horse's unease or, at the very least, was not doing anything productive to help him.

The rest of that summer, I tried to continue on the path that we had been traveling, pre-pregnancy, but after a while I started asking myself some familiar questions.

Was I having good days with Woody? Were there more good days than bad?

I had clung so tightly to the dreams and goals that I lost sight for a while that this was all supposed to be for fun and about the passion and love I felt for horses. It had become more frustrating and disappointing than relaxing and fulfilling.

With a year-old baby and life responsibilities, I didn't have the capacity that I used to have to give Woody the support he needed so that we could continue progressing together. I felt like a failure. How could other mothers work, raise kids, manage households and have the spare time, energy, and motivation to devote to horse care—let alone competitive riding?

I started grappling with the previously unimaginable idea that maybe I needed to sell Woody, and after a lot of consideration and tears, I posted a sale ad. There were no serious offers for the first month or so, and I continued to work with him.

By October, we were entering an annual clinic with world-class horseman Jim Anderson. At the end of our three days, I felt great about our progress, and Woody was as tuned in and willing as he had ever been. We had broken through the rough patch with consistency, determination, and hard work. Instead of throwing in the towel on progress after I had decided to sell him, I continued to show up, and eventually, our relationship returned to what it once was. The sale ad expired and I chose not to renew it.

The week after a Jim Anderson clinic leaves you feeling high on equestrian life and excited about future possibilities. This time though, after the clinic, I received a phone call from a lady wondering if Woody was still for sale and asking to come and try him out. I was on the rollercoaster of emotions and so caught off guard that I didn't know how to respond. Somewhat in shock, I agreed to let her come and see him.

The day of her visit, Woody charmed her with his sweet, adorable personality and athletic abilities. It was love at first sight, just as it had been for me. It wasn't long before I got the call with an offer, and knowing it was the right thing at the right time, I accepted.

Within a few weeks of having some of the best rides I had ever had on him, Woody was loaded onto a trailer to go live his new life. Just because you know you're making the right decision doesn't make it any easier. Even now, the emotions bubble over as I think back to that day and time.

I had held onto the fantasy of having my dream horse and achieving my goals with him for so long, and at the time, I worried that I was taking the easy way out. I sold my heart horse with the hopes of someday finding a different horse that enjoyed show life more and who would help me find my confidence again rather than needing me to provide that for him.

Looking back with a clear head and heart, four years later, I am content with my decision and so happy with life as it is now. The transition of being a struggling new mother, weighed down by real and perceived pressures, to a thriving mom of a five-year-old with two horses, two dogs, and two cats at home, plus a new equestrian business and a podcast has been a journey. I got to where I am now with the support of my husband, therapy, self-care—including more quality time with horses, a lot of books, and *finally*, a regular sleep schedule. The pieces have fallen into place.

Woody and I had so many experiences together, and the things that I did with him helped shape him into the wonderful partner he is for his current owner. Considering my mental and emotional state after having a colicky baby and trying to adjust to a new life and routine, I wish I had been easier on myself. If I were to relive it all, I would have taken competitions completely off the table. I would have ridden when I felt like it and spent quality time when I needed it.

Through the ups and downs of life, with and without horses, I've learned the importance of slowing down and appreciating what I have rather than adding pressure to achieve things on an arbitrary timeline. There seem to be some lessons in life that repeat themselves over and over until we truly get the message.

During the time of writing out this story, I have been in the process of preparing for my first reining competitions in over two years with my "new" horse Beau. You guessed it; the pressure is back on! Things have not exactly gone smoothly, the pandemic likely hasn't helped, and it would be so easy to fall into the trap of overwhelm, doubt, and self-pity again—but this time the lesson is fresh in my mind, and I'm ready to work through it all and to enjoy the ride!

About Nadine Smith

Nadine is likely to be one of the most enthusiastic and nerdy horse lovers in the room! She has had a lifelong passion for horses, with a strong interest in Western performance disciplines, equine behavior, and body language. Along with her husband, Nadine has lived in provinces all across Canada and has worked as a business management consultant for many years. She is the co-founder of Informed Equestrian and cohosts Canada Horse Podcast.

Nadine lives with her husband, son, and their four-legged family members in the Annapolis Valley of Nova Scotia on the property of her dreams.

Dedication

This story is dedicated to Mark and Anderson, the big human loves of my life.

Book Recommendations

You are a Badass: How to Stop Doubting Your Greatness and Start Living an Awesome Life by Jen Sincero

The Conscious Communicator: The Pursuit of Joy and Human Connection Inspired by the Art of Horsemanship by Nikki Porter
Horses Never Lie: The Heart of Passive Leadership by Mark Rashid

CHAPTER 11
UNSTABLE GROUND

BY MONTANA MADILL-LAYE

———

FOR AS LONG as I can remember and even before, horses have been a large part of my life. I was born and raised in Courtenay, British Columbia, on Vancouver Island, where my mom, a horse trainer, and my dad, a retired rodeo cowboy, owned a busy equestrian center together.

The farm, as it's known to our family, was my mom's childhood dream that, with help from my grandpa, became a labor of love for my parents in the '80s. With a twenty-four-stall main barn, 65x80 foot indoor arena, 160x200 foot outdoor arena, and fully functional rodeo grounds that sat on sixty-five acres, across from endless parks and trails—it was a little piece of horse lovers' paradise.

In all honesty, being raised in such an incredible place, how could I not have been a horse-crazy little girl? I just so happened to never grow out of it.

When I was younger, I was your stereotypical farm kid. I spent my days running around barefoot, building tree forts, catching salamanders, and spending a lot of time exploring the outdoors with friends. If I wasn't barefoot barrel racing around buckets in the back yard or roaming the neighborhood, the majority of my time was spent in the barn and arena, at local gymkhanas, jackpots, and eventually, rodeos.

Horses and the farm were my mom's business and livelihood, so there were strict rules and routines when it came to their care and wellbeing. They almost always took priority. When other families were going camping or taking family vacations, we were never too far from home, and if we were, the horses were in tow. I didn't always appreciate the lifestyle we lived because it interfered with "normal" kid things. I sometimes felt like I was missing out. As I got older, I started to realize how lucky I was and when I look back now, I am so grateful for the way I was raised. I learned so much from our way of life.

Although I wouldn't say it was typical, my childhood, as far back as I can remember, was pretty simple. Then at thirteen years old, my world changed overnight. That was the day childhood, as I knew it, came to an abrupt halt. I'll never forget it.

The day we found out that my father had been having an affair with my mom's best friend and business partner at the time, in a tack store they had just recently opened was the day it all changed. To complicate matters more, the woman he was having an affair with also happened to be my best friend's mom and my godmother.

We were heading home from a rodeo on the September long weekend when my mom called my dad to see what he was doing. He told her he was out for breakfast with "the friend." I can't remember if he was on speakerphone or my mom told us after, but when we heard that, my best friend and I looked at each other and rolled our eyes as if to say "Figures."

You see, prior to this, her daughter and my older sister had always said something was going on between our parents, but I'd refused to believe it. I don't remember ever seeing anything with my own eyes. Maybe it was because they were sneaky; maybe it was because I was naive, but eventually, as I got older and my sister and friends were persistent about the things they had seen, I started to see it as a possibility. At that moment, sitting in the back seat of the truck, not only did I finally see clearly what others had been seeing, but my mom did too.

The next few days are a bit of a blur. I remember my mom's friend coming over and talking to her, confirming that yes, it was true. She couldn't understand how my mom hadn't seen it sooner.

I remember listening from the basement as my parents argued once or twice, but overall, I don't remember being overly emotional. I think I was probably a little shocked. Being the people pleaser I was, I never really reacted and just tried my best to stay out of the way. I've always been pretty easygoing, so when I evaluate it now, I believe my lack of response was partly because of my personality but more so because at the time, I didn't understand the severity of the situation.

I guess I assumed things wouldn't change that much. I even told some friends, "It isn't a big deal: Lots of people's parents split up or get divorced, and it could be so much worse." Regardless of what I told myself, I never anticipated that the next fifteen years of my life would be completely engulfed by my parents' situation.

Since my parents owned the equestrian center together, they couldn't just go their separate ways. My dad had over eighty head of cattle on the property, my mom trained horses for a living, and they had both put over twenty-five years of blood, sweat, and tears into that place. Needless to say, neither one of them was keen on selling, and it left for a very complicated dynamic.

My dad rented an apartment in town, and I stayed with my mom on the farm. It started as a slow, drawn-out trickle of emotions from everyone involved. No one knew what to do, say, or how to act. Us kids, who prior to this had spent almost every day with each other, tried to keep things as normal as possible, but with the changed circumstances, they were never the same.

My parents tried to carry on with their separate lives but being that they had to see each other every day, it got complicated. One day they could be civil and friendly, and the next, it was WW3. There were your more "typical" fights, but then there were the next level, over the top, blow-ups.

We had an old bunkhouse building on the property from when my parents had run summer riding camps that was now used for storage. It was full of paperwork from the tack store they had owned, Christmas decorations, and other random house and horse stuff.

One day during one of their battles, my mom started throwing all of my dad's paperwork out into the driveway, which then enticed him to start up his tractor and drive it into the bunkhouse a couple of times, put it in park, and then leave. The bunkhouse would later be burned to the ground.

On another occasion, after who knows what provoked it, my mom

119

decided she would saddle up a horse, let all eighty cows out, chase them off the property, block the entrance with a truck and horse trailer, and then hide the keys so they couldn't be brought back on the property. She went in the back of a cop car—in her own words, "off to the clinker"—for her own protection.

We were a part of the equine and rodeo world, had three rental houses on our property, and had numerous boarders who were at the farm daily. As a kid, I loved growing up in what I considered our own little community but when shit hit the fan, living in a glass house was far from fun. To be honest, it was downright hard. And embarrassing.

While the other parties involved could step out of the spotlight and have a safe haven at home, we still had boarders, barrel races, barn dances, rodeos, and other events that took place on our property. It always felt like we had a magnifying glass on us, and the privacy to go through any kind of grieving process was non-existent. Even at school I couldn't totally escape it.

Once a girl in my Monday morning gym class asked me if everything was okay at home because she heard the cops had been dispatched to our farm on the weekend. I played it off like it wasn't our place they had come to because, of course I wasn't about to tell her the truth.

The truth was that my best friend Katherine, who was having a sleepover at the time, called the police on my dad because I couldn't bring myself to do it. He had decided bright and early on Sunday morning, before the rest of us were awake, that he needed to meet my mom's new boyfriend. He called from the barn, which gave us about one-minute warning before we could get up and get any of the doors locked. He came into the house and dragged mom's naked boyfriend out of the bed he was sharing with my mom. Katherine and I begged him to stop but he proceeded to beat him up out of jealousy. This is only one of many times the cops had to grace us with their presence.

Our family can now joke about the fact that our lives were reality TV-worthy, but as I was experiencing it, it was far from funny. I never knew what the days would bring, and things never settled down for long. Needless to say, trying to carry on a "normal" teenage life, when drama between my parents was a weekly occurrence, wasn't always easy and it all started to take its toll on me mentally.

I have two older half-siblings, but I'm my mom's only biological child, and when I saw how fragile she was through all of this, I felt the need to be there for her and tried to "fix" whatever I could. She is a very emotional woman, and during this time, she was perceived as "crazy" because she generally acted out of emotion without thinking of the consequence.

Often, I was caught in the crossfire and took the brunt of her displaced emotions. I saw her depression, anxiety, and loneliness, and I was constantly conflicted in my feelings. One minute I was her biggest supporter, and the next, I was being overwhelmed by her emotions and didn't know how best to handle situations that would arise. Between the wine and antidepressants, there were times she didn't leave her bed for days, and other times I wasn't always sure if she was going to be there at all when I woke up.

Once, after yet another fight, my mom had an emotional breakdown and disappeared. The farm is located across the road from a provincial park that has a river running through it. After looking around the property, someone noticed her car was down at the park without her in it. Knowing the mental state she was probably in, worry started to creep in. My mom cannot swim, and even though I didn't want to believe she would go to that extreme, I started to think the worst.

We started a ground search of the park, river, and surrounding area. After some time of searching with no luck, a helicopter was called in. We finally found her hiding in some thick bush, sobbing and saying how sorry she was. I was so furious with her for putting me through such an ordeal that I could barely even look at her, but the anger was quickly diluted with relief, seeing that she was alive and okay.

My dad, on the other hand, is a man of few words. He's quiet with his emotions and mostly slow to react, especially when he knows people are watching. To the public eye, he always seemed like the reasonable one. This often created a divide in our "community." Most people did not see the whole story. They sided with my dad. I saw both sides do and say ugly, hurtful things—things no child should have to witness or hear.

For over a decade, I tried my best to stay neutral, but looking back, I see that I felt robbed of my childhood. I felt I was the adult. Not only did I feel I had to be the mediator and peacekeeper in our family, but I also felt I had to defend them at every corner. There were very few places that I didn't feel like

I was walking on eggshells, waiting for the ball to drop, and it was completely exhausting.

Being a teenager during this struggle, I didn't know how to identify my feelings for what they were. Now I know there was very rarely a time I didn't feel a sense of stress or anxiety. I was experiencing trauma, and I coped by comparing my experiences to other people's. I constantly told myself that because I still had two parents, I was provided for and was still supported in the arena. "I didn't really have it that bad."

I knew it wasn't normal to be living in a constant state of worry, but I didn't know how to change it. Instead of asking for help or speaking my truth, I just put my head down, gritted my teeth, and hoped the storm would pass as quickly as possible. My siblings weren't really in the picture during this time, and I didn't want to burden my friends and other people with my problems, so I often spent time alone.

When my mom wasn't around, I'd have friends over, but rarely did I want to go out. I was always worried about what would happen if I left for too long, like I was the glue holding things together. My mind would race. Would my mom be okay? Would the horses get fed? Would the consequences or repercussions be worth it? It was a lot of responsibility for a teenager. This isn't something I told either of my parents or even close friends, but my horses heard a lot about it.

Throughout the years of dysfunction, one horse, in particular, carried a lot of weight for me. His registered name is Diamond Fritz Jet, but we affectionately call him Bynx. Looking back now, I realize just how much I owe to that horse.

My mom has always had a horse-buying addiction, and she bought him as a three-year-old shortly after my parents had split up. At first glance, he didn't look like much. He was a scrawny, underweight, average-looking sorrel gelding. A lot of people didn't know what she saw in him.

After only riding him from one end of an arena to the other, she felt something special, and he was heading home with us. At the time, I didn't think she needed another horse, but the universe knew otherwise. Although my mom did ride him a little in the beginning, from the get-go, it was evident—he was my horse.

At three years old, he had already been used as a team roping heel horse and was lightly started on the barrel pattern. Soon after we got him, we started our barrel racing journey together. Being that he was so young, we didn't expect to be competing with him for another couple of years, but as quickly as my mom had made the decision to buy him, he started to show some serious potential.

By the time he was four, I entered a few barrel races on him. Shortly after that, he started to win, so we tried our hand at some rodeos, and he won those too. He was a horse that you could do just about anything on. In high school rodeo, I barrel raced, pole bended, goat-tied, and breakaway roped off him. Then on a Monday morning, I could turn around and give a beginner riding lesson on him.

A few years into our journey, Bynx took me to the BC High School Rodeo Finals, to the BC Amateur Rodeo Finals numerous times, and filled my Canadian Professional Rodeo Association card. With him, I won my first, and so far only, professional rodeo. I don't think we knew the caliber of horse we had at the time, but I have always said if I knew then what I know now, I think he could have given me a shot at the Canadian Finals Rodeo.

From the day he came into my life, Bynx became my stable ground and safe place. He came into my world just as it was falling apart. It didn't matter if I was cleaning his stall or if we were out for a trail ride or running barrels; Bynx brought a sliver of peace to my otherwise chaotic existence.

Not only was he a distraction from the noise that I called my life, but it's when I could let the tears flow and the burden of the world roll off my shoulders. Almost the only times I felt a sense of calm was when I was with him. Whether it was at home or on the road when I buried my head into his neck to vent my hurt and frustration, he absorbed my emotions, and without judgment, he listened. Something I desperately needed, and I felt no one else in my world did.

For over eight years, during some of the most pivotal times of my life, when I didn't know how to ask for help, he was my rock and one of the only reliable things in my life. He must have known the baggage I was carrying, and how much I needed the stability he provided because he was always Mr. Dependable. If I needed to have an emotional meltdown in the corner of his stall while he gently sniffed my hair, to let me know he acknowledged my pain, or if I needed to win a cheque at the rodeo, there was never a time I felt he let me down in any kind of way. He always showed up with his whole heart.

Not only was he a safe space for me, but he also gave me hope that there was a way out of my situation. I wasn't stuck, and I didn't need to become a product of my circumstances. I had a lot of excuses to head down my own destructive path, but my parents, although haywire as hell at times, taught by example what hard work looks like and what you can accomplish when you're willing to put in the time and energy. Of course, I still did some typical teenage stuff, but I had goals, and they were always in the forefront of my mind. They were something positive to focus on and something I could actually control. If I didn't ride four to five times a week, I wouldn't be happy with myself because I felt I was letting my horse down.

When we went to jackpots or rodeos, I'd let my hair down and was social, but my horses were always my top priority. As Bynx and I grew as a team inside the arena and success came our way, I felt I had earned it, and it was something I could be proud of. It quieted the noise of our family chaos, and in those short-lived moments, I would feel content.

The dedication I had for my horse, and barrel racing, and the size of his heart took us all over BC, Alberta, and Washington. In 2008, at twenty years old, Bynx came with me to college in Altus, Oklahoma, where I joined the rodeo team. It was a terrifying, last-minute decision that ended up being one of the best decisions I've ever made.

At first, I didn't know how to be so far removed from my family and their issues. Often times I still got sucked into the drama even from thousands of miles away, but as the year went on, being away helped me to realize that their issues weren't mine to fix. I started to understand that their burdens weren't mine to carry, and everyone had to experience their own journey if they were going to heal. I was never going to be able to make them act or feel in certain ways, and in order to become my own person, I needed to be okay with that.

When I returned home from school, I got a job for a year, and then eventually, Bynx and I packed up yet again and moved to Alberta to rodeo and be with my now-husband, who I had met while in Oklahoma.

Moving to a new place, in the middle of nowhere, to live with a family I hardly knew wasn't easy, but as usual, Bynx was my pillar of support during our transition. There were times I felt homesick and missed my family, and there were other times I was grateful I wasn't there.

Regardless of wherever I was or what was going on, Bynx was a source of comfort. He felt like home to me, and I always appreciated having him with me. My parents gradually started to repair themselves and their friendship. Taking that time away and creating some distance, I learned not to carry so much of everyone else's burden. I slowly started to speak up and stand up for myself. If I needed to detach myself from a situation, I did. Eventually, I began to make myself and my happiness a priority.

Just like no two horses are the same, neither are we. All of us have a story, and every one of us experiences hard things in our lives. It's been a long and continuous journey, but I've started to understand that I don't need to compare my "hard" to anyone else's. There is no easy way to deal with hard things.

Although I often still struggle with it, I have learned that it's okay to talk about my situation and that some of the things I have been through are not normal or okay. Bynx helped me through the past but as I've grown older, I've learned that asking for help doesn't mean I'm weak and that everyone, at some point in their lives, needs someone else to depend on. Slowly, one day at a time, I've been able to acknowledge everything that's happened for what it was, and I've been able to start the healing process.

Without my horses—Bynx being at the forefront—and lessons they've taught and the opportunities they gave me, I feel like my journey to healing would have looked a lot different. I'm so grateful that through all of the highs, lows, ebbs, and flows, horses have saved me from some darker paths and helped shape me into the woman I am now. When I didn't know how to ask for help, they helped me. When I felt I had no one to depend on, they were dependable, and now at thirty-three years old, I can look back and thank these amazing creatures for helping me to cope during those hard times, to get past them, and to flourish. They taught me, among so many other things, the value of kindness, compassion, and hard work.

I try to embody these values daily and am relentlessly trying to pass those on to my daughter. Horses shaped the trajectory of my life. They are a daily reminder to show up with my whole heart and I truly don't know where I would be without them.

My mom's favorite quote and something she teaches others is "My horse, my teacher," by Alois Podhajsky. For me, this couldn't be more true. Whether it's in the arena or in life, I can undoubtedly say that my horses have always been some of my greatest teachers of some of life's greatest lessons.

Bynx, now twenty-one years young, is retired from competition and living his best life being "The King of the Ranch." He spends his days getting spoiled and teaching newcomers, mostly kids, how to ride. I can't say that they'll ever truly understand just how special he is, but I hope he gives the people he teaches even a sliver of what he gave me.

It hasn't been painless, but the harder I look at the whole situation, the better I've come to understand myself as a person, my past relationships, and, more importantly, what I want those to look like in the future. I know both of my parents made mistakes, as we all have, but as we continue to navigate our family's different dynamics, I've only grown closer to them. The pain has strengthened our bonds. Our relationships today are stronger than they've ever been. My parents are two of my best friends and biggest supporters in life, and for that, I am so grateful.

My story is one of self-dependence that led to self-discovery and acceptance. I hope that those who read it are reminded that regardless of circumstance, you can never truly understand what someone else is going through. Be unassuming and, more importantly, *be kind*. When life gets hard, never stop looking for the divine among the chaos because when it comes down to it, life is nothing but a beautiful mess.

About Montana Madill-Laye

Montana lives in Metiskow, Alberta, with her husband, daughter, and a handful of costly critters. She was born and raised on Vancouver Island in British Columbia and was lucky enough to grow up surrounded by horses. In her youth, she tried a number of different events, but rodeo and barrel racing became her focus and where her heart would remain. Over the years, whether through training, teaching, or competing, her horses have guided the trajectory of her life and helped her to become the woman she is today.

Dedication

This story is dedicated to my mom and every other person who has felt unheard or misunderstood while trying to navigate, survive, and thrive in this crazy thing we call life.

Book Recommendations

The Four Agreements by Don Miguel Ruiz
The Obstacle Is the Way by Ryan Holiday

Relentless by Tim S. Grover

CHAPTER 12
FULL CIRCLE
BY BETSY VONDA

—

ONE OF MY earliest childhood memories is standing with my arms wrapped around the front leg of our Quarter Horse, Bar. This likely happened when my mother's back was turned, and to her horror, as I was only five years old, and he was only a yearling. I am fortunate to have had horses as friends for as long as I can remember. I struggled with communication and making friends as a child, but my horses always welcomed me with a soft nicker. This relationship with horses would form me, challenge me, and in many instances, save me.

I am fortunate to have grown up in a horse-loving family. My parents split when I was eighteen months old, and even so, my mother did everything she could to keep her horse. Eventually, my sister and I got our own ponies. I've never known life without horses, and I am grateful for that. Looking back, I have always been drawn to them, to the point that I ran away from my grandmother when I was five years old at the Kingston Fall Fair. After a frantic search, they found me sitting on a pony at the petting zoo. His name was Smokey.

Smokey was almost thirty years old. He was a retired pony-rides pony and drifting from his prime. I'm told the petting zoo owner fancied my mother, and somehow, I came home with the pony. I'm pretty sure Smokey was just as happy about it as I was. He was a kind soul and went on to carry both myself and my stepbrother, Mitchell, to our first ribbons. He also was trained to drive, and I first learned to hitch all by myself with that sweet boy.

He would go all day when we began competing at the local club horse shows, from showmanship and western pleasure to trying his best at barrel racing. He lived out his days in our yard, picking at the grass and bathing in the sunshine. He had his own pony-sized stall at our small hobby farm outside of Lansdowne, Ontario.

One night, when he was about thirty-seven years old, we think he turned and hit his head; I still remember the sound of the vet laying him down in the trailer for his last sleep. I was nine at the time and will never forget the first loss of a family member. That pony taught me that horses will give you their heart and soul if you ask for it. I was an abrupt child, often tugging too hard and too quickly on the reins, but he tried for me and taught me to do better.

Living and growing up with horses at home would come to shape me as a person and my career path as well. Something that happened at that little hobby farm would be an incident I would later look back on when deciding to become a paramedic.

One day my sister and I got off the bus from school and found blood and broken glass at the front door of the barn. We opened the door to find my sister's pony standing loose in the aisle, covered in blood. Another horse had let her out of her stall, then let himself out of his stall, and she tried to jump out the barn window to escape him, unsuccessfully.

What I learned in those moments was that I could remain calm in the chaos. I was able to call for help, manage the horses, and provide initial care with my sister, all at the age of eight. However, I didn't realize until I was working as a paramedic that I was not only good at remaining calm in the chaos but that I had learned non-verbal communication from the horses and read the body language of those I met as patients and bystanders. These two skills have helped me time and again when working on the ambulance and helped me read situations that were about to turn violent. From horses, I learned how to diffuse situations and, in some cases, when to leave and create a safe distance before anyone got hurt.

When we moved to the hobby farm, I was in grade one and had to change schools. This was really hard on me because I struggled to be accepted and make new friends. Who knew children in grade one could have established cliques? I was so proud of my show clothes but quickly learned that it was not "cool" to wear them to school.

I have very few memories of grades one to seven when I left that school, but most of the ones I have are not pleasant. I often struggled to put my thoughts into words, resulting in violent outbursts and blackout moments of rage due to frustration. I struggled to communicate verbally with my family and with other children, yet, I didn't have to use words with my horses.

I couldn't wait to get home to spend time in the woods and hang out with my ponies. I used to spend hours just watching the herd interact. Horses offer us a judgment-free connection. I don't know how I would have survived my childhood without them and the great gifts they offered me.

I learned to connect and communicate with them, and through competition, I met other children who also loved their ponies and horses. I became friends with them quite easily, as we had a passion in common and could talk ponies all day long without missing a beat. My ponies, my horse show family, and the competitions gave me something to live for and a place to practice verbal communication.

We moved again during the summer of 2003 to just outside of the town of Napanee, Ontario, a month before I started grade eight. I remember being frustrated and wanting to graduate with the same group of kids I'd gone through elementary school with. In hindsight, I have no idea why, as I wouldn't call them my friends at the time. Of course, as it turned out, it was the best decision to move. I met real friends at my new school, and by this time, having horses was cool! We also moved to a bigger farm, with a large sand arena, a seven-stall barn, and a more competitive local horse show club.

In Napanee, horses harbored connection, and again I am forever grateful for that. One of the friends I made, Cassandra, got me to try out for rugby with her. I had no idea what it was, but I tried and made the team. Joining rugby taught me teamwork and introduced me to another level of work ethic and time management as I was still responsible for keeping two horses in shape.

For the first time in my life, I did something that terrified me. Rugby is a

131

tough sport! One of the people I met at high school was the first to plant the idea of being a paramedic in my mind, and being on the rugby sidelines, I got to chat with the local paramedic supervisor about what the job was really like.

This is one of the first chain reactions of saying "yes" to things that scare me and allowing those things to lead me to places I could never have imagined. This would become a common theme in my life, as I would be faced with many more terrifying yet pivotal decisions in the years to come.

Having joined a more competitive horseback riding club, we were encouraged by our new friends to come to some provincial-level competitions. We joined the National Barrel Horse Association (NBHA), the Ontario Barrel Racing Association (OBRA), and the Eastern Ontario Quarter Horse Association (EOQHA). Showing Quarter Horses was one of my mother's dreams. It also presented an opportunity that would change my life forever.

I earned enough points with EOQHA to make the National Youth Activity Team Tournament (NYATT) team, which meant my first trip to the All American Quarter Horse Congress in Columbus, Ohio. That was the world's largest horse show and I was thrilled to be competing there but never even dreamed of winning a class at that level of competition.

My horse, Cody's Curiosity, or Shugs as he was known around the stable, was just five years old. We'd bred and raised him, and he was the first horse I had trained myself from the start. As the season went on, he kept getting better and better at pole bending. The weekend before we left for Ohio, he won the NBHA/OBRA finals with a time of 20.6 seconds! A new personal best for both of us.

Off we went to Ohio, and I knocked poles in each of my youth classes, disqualifying me. The times I had run would have won the classes. I was very disappointed and discouraged, so I decided to practice before my last big run in junior horse pole bending.

While I was practicing, another girl approached and asked if she could work with me. We started chatting, and she asked if I would watch and see if I could help her figure out why she was knocking poles as well. Sure enough, I saw it. As it turned out, I was making the same mistake too! We worked through the solution together.

By helping her, I learned something new as well. This is one of those moments that sparked my passion for teaching and helping others. I am still grateful for this interaction. I went on to win the junior horse poles, my first Congress championship, and I couldn't have done it without that connection and conversation.

When I went to college to become a paramedic, I brought my horse with me. I knew that I would take a step back from competing once I graduated, so attending another Quarter Horse Congress was a must. I was only nineteen at the time and still struggled to control my emotions and environmental stressors.

This time with another season of competing under our belt, we went on to win two more pole bending championships and ran the second-fastest time of the Pole Bending Sweepstakes qualifying rounds. When it was then time for the sweepstakes final, the biggest run of my life at the time—in my nineteen-year-old mind—all hell broke loose.

The start time was changed. I couldn't find my hat strings because I had forgotten them at the photographers the night before. Then my lifeline, my blackberry, fell out of my golf cart. I had minimal coping skills at the time. I didn't know how to ground myself. I overrode my horse and knocked a pole. I was devastated.

On the drive home, we talked it out. I had let all these external factors affect me. Disrupt me. And so I began my journey to mindfulness.

As a paramedic, external distractions occurred on nearly every call. Tunnel vision is a common problem for students; often only seeing the patient and not necessarily taking in all the little details of the scene or even the other first responders. I still remember the first time it happened to me. I walked right past a firefighter who was approaching to report what had happened so far. I was staring at the patient and didn't even see him approaching me. I walked right past him. I had swung too far in the other direction, blocking out external distractions. The conversation that occurred after that call would plant another seed and influence my life forever.

I had two preceptors. Two paramedics had agreed to mentor me, Diane and Sarah, and they showed me how to really be a paramedic on the road, as we say, with real patients. They taught me we are really like detectives. We need to take in all the information we can, not only how the patient presents, but the environment we find them in, and the things they've told the other responders and their families. I needed to not let it sway me either. It is all information that can help me think critically and clearly and keep me safe.

They also taught me not to take anything the patient says to me, such as insults, personally. That person is reacting because of their current situation and past experiences. They only see the uniform, not necessarily the person in it. This advice trickled over into my personal life and horsemanship as well, even though it took me many years to realize it.

When I graduated, I was hired by the Ottawa Paramedic Service, which was another one of those terrifying-yet-do-it-anyway decisions I had to make. At the time, I was working for the Halton Region Paramedic Service and loved it there. The nation's capital is a big service, with high profile calls and people. I was twenty-one at the time, and all my friends were attending university in Ottawa. So, I said. "Heck yes, let's do it!"

Ottawa was an adventure I'll never forget. I learned to stand on my own two feet. I made new friends, learned to be okay on my own, and tasted life without horses. What I learned about myself was that I needed to have goals. I had settled into my career, had a great man and a great dog. But having left the horses back at home in Napanee, with no immediate plans to move them, I found myself lost. I had so many wonderful things going for me, yet I was coming home irritable and restless.

My boyfriend suggested I come to the gym with him. He was a bodybuilder and started to teach me the importance of nutrition, because I lived on junk food, and how I could shape my body with weight training. What I didn't expect when I started down this journey was the mental growth I would experience. I jumped in with both feet, trying to learn as much as possible about fitness training and nutrition.

I quickly learned another level of discipline, consistency, long-term view, and letting go of self-judgment. Each weight I lifted required my focus and attention. I learned to connect with each muscle in my body. I learned how what I ate influenced not only my body but also my mind. I learned to find balance as I swung too far at one point and began demonizing certain foods. I did compete in a fitness competition and found it was too unhealthy for me. I began to focus on learning how to help my body run as efficiently as possible instead.

This new perspective also came with me into my work with horses. I became a more aware rider, with a greater connection to each muscle in my body and how my movements in the saddle affected them, positively or negatively. I realized that horses often matched my energy around them and that I should not assume and judge their behavior but try to understand what may be out of balance and influencing them. I now help horses find the balance that I strive for every day.

After my relationship ended, I became close friends with a wonderful woman I worked with, Anouk. Anouk introduced me to yoga. She taught me the importance of self-care and friendship. It was in 2013 that I began my journey with yoga, and I have never looked back. Yoga reminded me that there is no power in judgment, of self or others, and that movement with breath is as powerful as medicine. I began to see the parallels in horse training as well: how to find ease in the effort, how we can take in information without judgment, how to be empathic to the horse, and take nothing personally. Also, I recognized the power of holding space in time for ourselves and our horses.

After five long years away from horses, I was asked to start coaching at a barn outside of Ottawa. I knew then I needed to bring my horse back into work and return to competition. I found a great barn and started training again. I bought a little two-horse trailer and upgraded my jeep to pull it. We had started our season and were finding our groove when I hit my head one night coming out of the ambulance, suffering my first concussion.

At the time, I struggled to accept this. I didn't lose consciousness; I'd bumped my head before and never gotten sick. I felt weak, and my head hurt, but I struggled to accept that I was concussed and injured. Over the next few days, I became sicker and sicker, to the point I had tunnel vision, slow speech, nausea, and severe sensitivity to light and sound. I had to have a friend drive me to get groceries. When I went to the doctor to extend my time off work, I started bawling uncontrollably in the waiting room when they told me they might not be able to complete my paperwork at that clinic. That was definitely not normal for me.

I booked an appointment with my chiropractor, and luckily, he had completed many courses in concussion management. He defined what kind of "rest" I needed to do; brain rest and to give myself grace, as this was not going to heal overnight. He explained how dangerous it would be for me to be riding, that a fall and second hit to the head could kill me. At that time, it was hard to believe until someone sent me an article about a young rugby player and how she died on the field, in Ottawa, following another hit to the head while she was already concussed.

I accepted that my riding season was over. I needed to focus on healing if I ever wanted to ride again. It took me eight weeks to recover from my first concussion, and unfortunately, it wouldn't be my last. There were two more concussions to come, and both from hitting my head on the ambulance. As it turns out, where I hit my head the first time affected my peripheral vision. I knew what to do to recover, but in hindsight, I recovered only to about 80% of normal. After my third hit, my recovery plateaued. I had enough trouble with my vision that it wasn't safe for me to return to the ambulance or compete at the level I used to. My brain couldn't keep up!

By this time, I had joined my now-husband, Blake, in Barrie, Ontario, and was working for a new paramedic service. I was encouraged to apply for a position as an acting trainer but would have to be fully cleared to take on the new role. I experienced my first severe episode of post-concussion syndrome when writing my cover letter to apply for the new position. I had pushed my brain too hard and was experiencing severe symptoms.

This was when I got a message from a fellow barrel racer, Amanda, who suggested I see an osteopath. I was desperate to feel better, especially now that I was experiencing intrusive thoughts, telling me to sell my horse as I would never ride again. *Terrifying!*

I went to see my first osteopath, and the treatment gave me my life back! I woke up the next day, normal. And I don't say that lightly. He had found many restrictions in my fascia and released them, returning my circulation and breathing to normal. I was cleared to return full duties after only three treatments. I got my life back and learned that osteopathy was not only for humans but also for horses.

It would come full circle as I began to compete again and was preparing Shugs for one more Congress, almost ten years later. He had come up subtly lame after our first two competitions in 2018. I have never dealt with a lameness that was not from an acute, apparent injury before. The vets assessed him and thought he'd suffered a bone bruise.

With rest and a slow return to activity, we finally competed again at the end of August. I had started to notice behavior I'd never seen from him before. He developed severe separation anxiety when he wasn't with Blake's new horse. He would work himself into a sweat and try to jump out of the stall kind of bad! *Odd*, I thought to myself. I had raised this horse and never witnessed this type of behavior from him before.

A month before Congress, at the NBHA finals, Shugs ran his heart out and won us the pole bending title, running the fastest time he'd run in ten years! But when he sat for the final turn, he took a funny step and became a bit off in the hind end. The same friend and osteopath, Amanda, who had suggested I get treated by one, was at this barrel race. She treated him and suggested I contact Kayte Armstrong, a fellow osteopath and now professor of the program, who had just moved to Barrie.

Kayte helped both of us prepare for another Congress, which we attended and redeemed ourselves! We finished fifth in the final sweepstakes and placed seventh overall in the average. That would be Shugs' final run. When we returned home, I got a second opinion as he still wasn't himself, and he was diagnosed with navicular. At the age of eighteen, I decided to retire him.

I was in a place in my life where I was able to see his retirement as the best decision for him and as an opportunity for me to make a connection with a new horse. I truly believe that everything happens for a reason. Going down the rabbit hole into the causes, presentations, behaviors, and influences on subtle lameness, I stumbled upon a fellow named Warwick Schiller on YouTube.

Warwick had also started down a different path with his horses, one of listening to them and changing the way he looked at things. He inspired me to try a new way of interacting with and training horses. I had started to understand the connection between behavior changes in the horse and the pain they experienced. This also led to me many resources that discussed other causes of undesirable behavior. I learned to look at the horse's behavior with empathy, not judgment, and try to resolve their pain, meet their needs, clarify communication, and help them feel safe.

Over the last four years, horses have come into my life that have helped me explore, refine, and further deepen my ability to listen, connect, hold space in time, and help them heal. All the while doing this same work on myself and evolving the relationships with those around me. It's been scary at times, stepping away from the conventional, trusting my gut, connecting with my intuition. Still, it has also led to the most moving and most significant experiences of my life.

All of the events, people, and challenges I have shared with you have led me here, to this moment, typing these words on this page. Horses have been the constant catalyst to all of the greatest and most challenging things in my life thus far. I hope they have been the same for you, each in their unique ways.

I have one simple request for you. Take a few moments and reflect on your life with horses thus far. The lessons, the challenges, and the ways they may have shaped you. Together, let's be grateful for them, and how they've brought us together through these words and for the moments they will continue to create for us in the future.

About Betsy Vonda

Betsy is an equine advocate, performance and behavioral consultant, trainer, coach, clinician, and barrel racing competitor based out of Barrie, Ontario, Canada. She supports the County of Simcoe Health and Emergency Services Division as an Education Coordinator and Primary Care Paramedic.

Betsy spends her days developing and delivering education for paramedic services, long-term care staff, and local fire departments. On evenings and weekends, she can be found with horses and their people, broadening their communication and understanding of each other. She is a passionate yogi, health enthusiast, and skier. She is loved and supported by her husband Blake and dog Humphrey.

Dedication

I dedicate this chapter to my mother, Barb, my sister Sarah, and my husband, Blake. They are my constants, my guiding lights, my biggest fans, and my supporters. I wouldn't be the person—especially the horse person—I am today, without each of them.

Book Recommendations

Relational Horsemanship by Josh Nichol
Listen Like a Horse - Relationships Without Dominance by Keri Lake
Finding the Missed Path- The Art of Restarting Horses by Mark Rashid
A Horseman's Pursuit - joshnichol.com by Josh Nichol

CHAPTER 13
HEART OF STEELE

BY TERESA ALEXANDER-ARAB

—

I TELL PEOPLE THAT I have spent my entire life building a path to horses. It has neither been smooth nor easy, and yet I never wavered in my goal. When I am separated from horses for any length of time, I start to feel like a vital piece of me is missing. I don't remember a time when I wasn't drawn to horses.

When I was three years old, I often stayed with my grandparents in the country. Next door, there were horses out in the pasture. When unsupervised, I would make my way over there.

One day the neighbor brought me home and yelled at my mother: "I found her in the horse pasture again. It's not safe!"

My mother thanked him and then, after he left, told me that I was not to ever go there again.

"Why do you go there?" my mother asked with tired eyes.

I answered, in my three-year-old's innocence, "I talk to the horsies."

I finally had an opportunity to learn ride in my early twenties and I spent the next forty years of my life building my life around horses. After beginning riding lessons, I never looked back. I was fully committed. When money was limited, I would work at the stable in exchange for rides. I even talked my husband into spending money on purchasing my first horse rather than buying furniture for our new home. My family and I were living in town, and I boarded my horse, but my dream was to have my own property. I wanted to be able to go out and be with my horses, not just ride.

When I was in my mid-forties, and the children had left for university, we put the house on the market and started looking for a country property. The realtor stopped trying to get me to look at the house first, knowing that I would inspect the property and barn primarily. Many times I didn't look at the house at all because I knew it wasn't for us as soon as I stepped onto the property. If the property wasn't suitable for my horse, the house was not suitable for us. I looked at so many places that I lost count.

Finally, I came to a twenty-acre property just outside of town. It had no barn, but the land was perfect. I walked into the house and, while it was clearly showing its age, I could see the potential. Then I looked outside the window and saw this huge oak tree in the front yard. I turned to the realtor and said, "We'll buy it!"

"Don't you want to get Ed's opinion?" the realtor said with some hesitation.

"I will show it to him, but we're buying it," I replied with total confidence.

We bought the house, but we had to spend the first year renovating it, rather than living in it. We moved in and then started on my real priorities: building the barn, putting in paddocks, and constructing the riding ring. I was meticulous about all of it. I rejected several contractors because they did not talk to me or respect my opinion. I found one who just nodded and agreed, when I said, "Any decisions that need to be made are mine. You can talk to Ed, but if I get home and disagree, you are changing it." And he was as good as his word.

As soon as my barn and paddock were built, I brought home my horse— an older gelding named Irish who had some soundness issues. I was in my mid-forties, and it felt like I was twelve again and living my dream. Well, most of it. There was just one more piece missing.

I'd always wanted to buy a young horse and raise it myself. I had previous experience in purchasing a two-year-old and a three-year-old, but never a baby. I made a list of what I wanted. Okay, truth be told, I made multiple lists. The first one was a list of favorite breeds. I had decided I wanted a warmblood. I spent a long time looking, and it seemed that there was always something not quite right.

So, I made changes to my list and finally arrived at my final list:

1. Gelding. I already had a gelding, and it seemed easier to have two.
2. Between 15.3 and 16.2 hands high. I didn't need a giant of a horse.
3. Temperament was key. I wanted a sensible and brave horse. One who could be taken into new situations without freaking out.

My other list was what I wanted to do with this horse:

1. Ride dressage.
2. Hack out. This was a must. I love to ride in the woods and trails.
3. Show, but this was a small piece. I would show to have fun and see how I'm doing.
4. Go to clinics and other events.

I was starting to get frustrated in my search when a friend, Karen, contacted me. At that time, she was breeding Andalusian horses, and they had a young colt for sale. She thought I should come and look. I decided to go but didn't really think I wanted a Baroque style of horse. And I *definitely* didn't want a gray. The idea of grooming a gray horse with a long mane filled me with horror. I went to look anyway. To my surprise, I fell in love. His temperament seemed to suit me to a T, and I liked his movement.

Karen let me ride her Andalusian mare; I was impressed. Not only was she comfortable, but she was so tuned in, really trying to figure out what I wanted. I went home and reflected and asked to go back for a second look.

This time I dragged my husband, Ed, along with me. I liked the colt even more the second time. I decided to make the purchase. His name was DC Acero. Acero is Spanish for Steele, and so that became his barn name.

Irish took to Steele like he was his mother. It was adorable to see him watch Steele like a hawk. It felt like we were both raising him.

Having horses at home is very different than boarding. It was like I was three again and spending time sitting in the pasture "talking to horses" only without anyone stopping me. When I started to ride Steele, it felt like all my childhood dreams had come true. I used to joke that I was two people. The professional who made decisions, worked on policies, and supported my staff at work, and within five minutes of coming home, I turned into the horsewoman, who threw hay bales, mended fences, and drove a tractor.

No matter how stressful my workday was, I could feel it melt away as soon as I changed out of my professional clothes and into torn denim and flannel. The farm, and in particular the barn, was my refuge. I would spend hours puttering away and feeling that deep contentment that only comes from doing what you truly love.

I had a lot of adventures raising and backing Steele. He truly was my "heart horse." I loved the bones of that horse. He wasn't always easy, but he tried. He was curious and always wanted to be around us. We used to have to keep watch on our tools because he would steal them and run around the field. When I was anywhere nearby, he would blow in my ear as though to say "Come and play with me." When I would turn him out into the field after working with him, he would follow me back to the barn wanting to do more.

The first time I took him off the farm to a clinic, he was a star. I remember my feelings of pride when the clinician, a well-known judge and dressage trainer, said, "He is a wonderful horse. He has good movement, and he has a fabulous mind."

And then the worst nightmare of any equestrian happened, right in my own backyard. In a horrible, tragic, *senseless* event, Steele, my childhood dream, died.

On a crisp morning in December, I came out of the house and saw two strange dogs in my yard. I looked in the field and saw Irish running frantically in the paddock and Steele in the neighbor's field. I screamed for Ed, grabbed a halter and lead, and took off running.

I called for Steele, and he saw me, but one of the dogs went after him, and he bolted again. I watched helplessly as he ran through a fence and got caught. He pulled himself free, ran into a swamp, and fell. As I ran up to him, I could see that he was totally panicked. I put on his halter and spoke soothingly to him. He tried to get up but fell. I desperately watched as he fell, over and over. Finally, he stopped trying and just lay in the muck and let the water come over his head.

Ed caught up to me, and I told him to call the fire department and the vet and put Irish in his stall. He ran back to the house while I desperately tried to keep Steele's head above the water. I have never felt so helpless or so alone.

I realized that his hind leg was trapped in the swamp under some branches and muck. I tried to free his legs from the branches. He lay perfectly still whenever I was around his legs, only trying to get free when I stepped back.

I could see that Steele was going into shock, and his efforts to save himself were becoming weaker. He started to tremble and close his eyes. The entire time the dog was circling us, not barking or playing, but watching us.

It felt like a century, but the fire department finally arrived. I ran to the trucks. "Get some ropes, blankets, and a shovel!" I ordered. With their help, we were able to get Steele's legs free, but he was unable to stand. The dog kept coming closer, and I asked one of the firemen to handle it. The dog disappeared.

After an incredible ordeal of wedging tires under his back and getting a rope around his body, we got Steele to his feet. He walked forward but couldn't put weight on his right front leg. He stood there, covered in sticky, awful mud and shaking. I put a blanket over his back as I saw the vet approaching.

She examined him and, with compassion, said, "I'm very sorry, but your horse has broken his humerus."

I looked at her with a blank expression. "He'll have to be put down?" I questioned, hoping she would say no and that there was a path out of this nightmare.

"Yes," she answered.

As I turned away, the guy who owned the dog who chased Steele arrived and was looking directly at me.

"You killed my horse!" I heard myself scream.

All he could say was, "I'm so sorry."

"*YOU KILLED MY HORSE! YOU KILLED MY HORSE!*" I couldn't stop screaming it as I advanced on him.

Ed caught up to me and grabbed me. I collapsed to the ground, screaming. I was making a hysterical spectacle of myself, and I didn't care. I screamed at the universe. I couldn't breathe. I still cannot describe the depth of pain and rage I was feeling in that moment. It was swallowing me whole. I could feel

Ed holding me, and it seemed like he was an anchor holding me to the earth.

Then, I took a shuddering breath, and I got up. I walked to Steele, who looked at me with such pain and confusion. My heart broke even more. I wrapped my arms around his neck.

"I'm sorry. I'm so sorry. I should have protected you. I'm sorry. I love you." I said it over and over. I didn't care who heard.

Ed helped Steele keep his head up, and three firemen helped him to stay upright. I will always remember how they gave what they could to support an animal they didn't know so he wouldn't suffer as much.

The vet explained that she would sedate him and then administer the dose to send him on his way. She said that he might react badly and that I did not have to stay.

"I'm staying," I mustered the strength to say.

She questioned my decision, "Are you sure?"

"Yes." I had never been so sure.

The vet sedated him, and slowly the pain faded from his eyes. Then I noticed that I was experiencing the very thing I had just witnessed and talked my horse through. I was in shock, and my body was shaking uncontrollably. The vet administered the injection. He fell softly to rest. I held his head until his eye showed that his soul was gone.

Ed walked home with me, and arrangements were made to pick up his body and bring him home. I walked along the road, and my regular vet pulled up because he had heard what happened and drove out to check on me.

"Get in," he instructed.

All I could reply with was, "No."

"Get in."

I could tell no was not going to be accepted. So I did get in, and he enfolded me in his arms, and I broke down again. He drove us home, and I got out. I went right to the barn to check on Irish. He was upset but uninjured. I wrapped my arms around his neck, and he, too, wrapped me in an embrace.

I went into the house and got into the shower. I huddled on the bottom of the shower floor, sobbing uncontrollably with the water washing away the tears that poured out of me.

When I got out of the shower, I looked out the window and saw Steele's body where they had placed him to be buried. I ran out and asked the man in the backhoe to stop. I put a halter on Irish and brought him outside. He was agitated but walked beside me, and we stopped together and looked at Steele. I stood there with him while he reached forward with his nose and blew gently on his leg. He gave Steele a nudge and then looked at me. He knew his friend was gone.

The day that Steele died changed me forever—in ways I could never have foreseen. For days I couldn't even leave the house. I walked around in a daze. I couldn't work or sleep. Every time I closed my eyes, I saw the horrific events again and again.

My friends were amazing, and all of them reached out to support me as best they could. No one said, "It was just a horse," and for that, I would be forever grateful. For weeks I would drive to work going out of my way, so I wouldn't have to drive by the spot where I lost my heart horse. Every day at the end of my driveway I would say to myself, "You can do this," and then turn the opposite way.

Irish grieved as well. He wouldn't eat and would stand as close to Steele's grave as he could during the day. It was heart-breaking to witness a horse feeling the loss I, too, was experiencing. My vet loaned me one of his horses as a companion which helped Irish overcome his sadness.

In hindsight, I realize now that I was in shock and suffering from PTSD, but I didn't recognize it then. All I knew was that I was filled with uncontrollable anxiety when the horses were home without anyone there. I would drive home repeating over and over, "They are fine," until I pulled in the driveway and saw that they were, in fact, fine.

I felt lost. In the past, the barn had been my refuge. It was the place I went to when I needed to restore my soul. I could find comfort in simple tasks like sweeping a floor, cleaning a water bucket, and organizing tack. I loved the smells of the hay, shavings, and horses. The sounds of horses eating always brought a smile to my face and a feeling of peace in my heart.

When Steele died, the barn became a place of pain, not of solace. I felt like I was spinning because the first place I would normally head to feel better was ripped away from me. I would go to the barn, only do what needed to be done, then head back to the house.

I learned that grief could come in waves and touch everything you love, but that doesn't mean that all joy is gone. I think it was beneficial that I still had to go to the barn to do chores. I would make myself stay and do small chores like grooming the horses, tidy the tack, and sweep up old hay. Slowly I found myself start to find ease in the simple chores. The horses were soft and gentle with me. I think we worked together to help each other.

I knew that I couldn't keep my loaned horse, Lexie, forever. As I was mourning the loss of Steele, I was also mourning all that we weren't going to be doing. It felt unbearable. I could not see myself without horses, but I also couldn't bear to think of replacing Steele. *How would that even be possible?* I was feeling torn and confused. Ed encouraged me to consider another horse, not to replace Steele, but to have something to look forward to. He believed that if I had a horse to work with, I would begin to heal.

Then, one night, I had a dream. I was in the middle of some forgettable dream when I was suddenly in a small clearing in the woods. It was night, and Steele was grazing there. He saw me and said, "Oh, hi. There you are." I stayed there with him for a while, and then I started to walk away. Steele followed me as we walked through the street of a small town and past fields. I thought that he would leave me, but he didn't. I decided that if he followed me, I would take him away from there. I reached my trailer, but it had been partially dismantled. Steele watched as I tried to fix it.

"I don't think I can come with you." I heard him say.

I quickly replied, "Yes, you can. I'll get this fixed, and we can go."

He watched me quietly, and I finally got it back together. I turned to him, and he said, "I can't come with you."

I started to cry, and then he blew in my ear like he always did. "Goodbye."

And he was gone, and I was awake.

A friend with a profound spiritual gift helped me to interpret this dream: The trailer was a metaphor for how I wanted to fix what happened but could not. "He knows you will use what you learned in your earthly journey together, and he will be with you as you move forward."

A few days later, I started to click on horse ads. I could only look for a few seconds at some horses before I had to stop looking at them all together because they reminded me too much of Steele. However, I kept going back and clicking, and it became easier. And that was how I found myself on a plane with my good friend Karen to go to look at some horses for sale in Virginia.

We had three horses to check out. All of them were well-bred, young Andalusians. One was a gelding that reminded me very much of Steele, but there was one particular mare that pulled at my heart. Karen said that the minute I sat on her, I started to smile. I felt like I had come home. She was young, sensitive, and beautiful. Her name was Charlante. The breeder had sold her then she passed through a couple of hands, being returned as "being unsuitable for FEI competition." Since I had no intention of competing internationally, that was not a deal-breaker for me. I made arrangements for a vet check, insurance, and transportation to Canada.

That winter was one for the record books. There was so much snow in Nova Scotia that many roofs collapsed under the weight. Having a horse being shipped during that time was nerve-racking, but Charlante finally arrived safely. Shortly after she came home, I settled on a barn name for her: Carmen. It completely suited her look and temperament.

Carmen was very different from any horse I had ever ridden. She was sensitive, reactive, and had very little interest in people. When I started riding her, the wheels quickly came off the bus. She had zero interest in listening to my aids, and when she was unsure of what I was asking, her go-to response was to spin and bolt. And she was unsure *a lot*.

I initially had the confidence that I could ride it out and get to the other side. I was wrong. It seemed that nothing I would do worked for any length of time to help us come together; it was like trying to break through a concrete wall. We'd have some good rides, and then the wheels would fall off again.

I tried to get some help, but it was impossible to find anyone in my area, and no one wanted to drive that far. I did everything I knew how to do. The best advice I had, came from a classical trainer from Spain who was in my area giving a clinic and came to help me. She kept trying to tell me that it was my own tension and emotion that was getting in the way. I literally did not know what she was talking about. I believed that I was being strong and not afraid. We did make progress while she was here, but I realize now, it was not sufficient for me, given where I was emotionally.

A year later, after one incredibly difficult ride, I dismounted in tears. I knew I had to get help, yet all the doors I tried knocking on were locked. I wondered if I had made a mistake. I know I was not alone in this and that many people thought I had the wrong horse and that I should sell her. To this day, I cannot give you one logical reason why I did not sell my mare and move on to another horse. What I can tell you is that something broken in Carmen was speaking to what was broken in me. Giving up on *us* seemed to be giving up on *myself*. I decided to contact a local Western trainer for help.

As an English rider, it seemed strange to ask a non-dressage trainer for help. But hiring the Western trainer opened my eyes to a whole new way of doing things. I learned a lot about groundwork and how to be clear in what I wanted. During this time, I also started to piece together some of Carmen's history.

Carmen was born in Virginia and had sold as a weanling to a breeding program in Michigan. They then sold her as a two-year-old to someone in Texas. She was backed at three years old, which for an Andalusian is far too early. I do not think that Carmen was abused in the traditional sense, but knowing her as I do, I believe that she was backed without sensitivity or the chance to learn what was wanted. Her reaction to side reins indicated that she had been tied into a frame. As I have said, Carmen is a very sensitive, reactive horse, and backing a horse like this requires time, tact, and gentleness.

At some point in her training, she was taken on a hack and had a wreck, falling into a ditch. That was when she was returned to her breeder. Carmen had one answer to pressure—to spin and bolt. She literally did not know that there were other options. Teaching her that there were better ways to handle pressure was an uphill battle. Our progress was definitely not linear. Some days I was sure we were on the right path, and on others, I was convinced that it was hopeless.

I learned a lot from that trainer, but I was still missing an important element; I wanted a relationship with Carmen, not *just* an obedient horse. Over the next few years, I found myself learning from anyone who would teach me, in-person and online. I attended a trail clinic that opened my eyes to how to break down a task so that each step made sense. I found a dressage coach to improve my riding skills. As our training began to fall into place, it was clear that something was still not quite right. Finally, and, regrettably, not as soon as I wish I could have discovered it. I learned of and began treating Carmen for stomach ulcers.

There was a remarkable change, and riding began to be fun after that. I continued to work on my riding and honing my groundwork skills. I became better at reading her body language and recognizing the pressure I put on her.

I also was working on myself as a means to better our relationship together. I began learning who I was and what I had been ignoring for most of my life. If I were a horse, you would say that I was shut down. I realized that I had invested a lot of energy into denying my anxiety and other negative emotions.

Once I recognized why I was doing that, I started making different choices. It was not easy, and I failed a lot, but as I moved through it all, I became more congruent about who I was. I also began to realize that Carmen was reacting to the lack of agreement between how I presented myself and how I truly felt. I would tell myself I was fine even though I was frankly terrified that she was going to bolt, and I would get hurt. I would act calm even though I was unhappy. I had recurring nightmares of the horses being loose and not being able to catch them. I wasn't depressed or unhappy all the time, but I was not in touch with who I was, and I was definitely not comfortable with that person.

As I became more open about how I was feeling, Carmen became more interested in me as a partner. I learned not to let my emotions be decided by how she was feeling. Instead, I became a mentor that could show her how to be okay. I learned how to draw a line and stick to it with firmness, not anger. Most importantly, I stopped wishing that Carmen was a different horse and let myself love her for who she was; a dramatic, opinionated, sensitive, and beautiful mare. I also stopped waiting for the "movie moment" and became content with the small steps. Every bad ride was not a disaster, and every good ride didn't mean we were perfect. Perhaps the biggest lesson was being okay with not being perfect.

One beautiful summer evening, I was cleaning stalls and left Carmen's door open. This was not a new thing, but this time Carmen walked out and headed toward the door. I gently walked and picked her halter while she looked out the door toward the road. I knew that if I hurried or reacted, she would be gone out the door. Instead, I stood there, breathing quietly and speaking to her gently. She looked out the door and then turned and walked back to her stall. I walked up and rubbed her shoulder. "Thank you for not leaving," I said to her. She blew in my hair and then turned to eat her hay.

About Teresa Alexander-Arab

Teresa grew up in Nova Scotia where she developed a love of animals and literature. She works in health care and is a regular contributor to a *Maritime Horse and Pony*, and has an online blog called *Journey with a Dancing Horse*. She spends her free time (and money) on her horses, reading, and exploring the countryside. A passionate horse person, she constantly strives to improve her knowledge and understanding. She believes that not only can horses show us who we are, but they can help us be better people—as long as we are able to listen. Teresa lives on a small farm in rural Nova Scotia with her two horses, a dog, a cat, a flock of chickens, and her husband.

Dedication

This chapter is dedicated to my husband, Ed, who has never faltered in supporting my love of horses. Despite not being a horse person, he has pounded fence posts, repaired the numerous things horses like to break, and has taken care of them when I could not. As I struggled through my grief and loss, his love and kindness helped me in ways I cannot describe. He is my best friend, my hero, and my love.

BOOK RECOMMENDATIONS

The Confident Rider Podcast by Jane Pike
Dare to Lead by Brené Brown
Dressage Naturally by Karen Rohlf

CHAPTER 14

THROUGH THEIR EYES

BY BRIANNA GRAHAM

—

MY OWN JOURNEY to healing revolves around an anxious runaway mare who had yet to become the solid and dependable herd leader she is today. Mocha would eventually find confidence under saddle with a soft and relaxed rider, but not without sending that same rider over the fence in fits of anxiety first. Mocha gave me purpose and the motivation I needed to take my anxiety, depression, and ADHD seriously for the first time in my life.

While in my first year of graduate school, and at the height of my mental health issues, I used my student loan and impulsively bought the sweetest, most personable buckskin that I had been training for future use in a lesson program. Little did I know this golden horse would both transform me as a horsewoman and heal parts of me that had been broken long before she walked into my life.

But first, to begin, we have to back up a little bit. I've ridden, trained, and worked with horses my whole life. When I was thirteen, I switched disciplines from English to Western. I was offered the opportunity to help restart a little mare named Krissy. Krissy had a questionable past that led to her lack of trust in humans and often dangerous reactions to the world around her. Krissy was a hot-headed firecracker with a knack for gymkhana and team cattle penning.

She was guarded, emotionally, and was not sensitive to her rider's emotions. She had started to come around, in her later years with me, but she was her own horse with her own agenda.

During my middle and high school years, I suffered silently from anxiety and depression. I spent many hours crying into her mane, and Krissy was always there for me on my bad days. At that point, the mental health campaigns to break the stigma attached to mental illness did not exist. If I dared to share how I felt, it was always brushed off by my peers. I always felt alone. I had a lot of friends, but the demons in my head convinced me that no one cared. I had Krissy, though, and she offered me comfort, love, and a home in a world where my demons would have me believe I did not belong.

When I went off to university, facing the world without Krissy was more difficult than I had ever imagined. I had gone across the province for school and could no longer run to the barn and bury my head in her neck when my depression or anxiety overcame me. I had a lot of difficulties making new friends at school, and I recall a time I went two weeks where I did not speak to a soul other than my parents over the phone. I cried every day from loneliness and wished I could escape to see my horse so she could remind me that I was worthy.

My second year away at school was harder than the first. It wasn't until then that I was formally diagnosed with Generalized Anxiety Disorder, Panic Attack Disorder, Major Depressive Disorder, and Insomnia. After spending many hours with a therapist, it became clear that I had suffered from all of these mental illnesses from the age of six, unknowingly using my bond with animals as a very successful coping mechanism.

During university, I did not give up riding, and I went to another barn to learn more about starting young horses and reining from a highly regarded coach in my hometown. Although I was having a lot of fun riding highly skilled horses, I lacked the bond with them that I had with Krissy.

Around that same time, I became involved in my first serious relationship, and my constant feeling of loneliness and insomnia seemed to have been cured. I continued to suffer from anxiety and Imposter Syndrome, particularly around school and while riding at this new barn on highly skilled horses.

My happiness depended on my relationship, and at any sign of trouble, my mood would drop, and the feelings of loneliness and worthlessness would come rushing back. At one point, when things were not working out, I found myself in the midst of a depressive episode and at my lowest.

Heavily encouraged by my parents, I sought help from my family doctor. Where I had been struggling with the ongoing tug of war of whether or not to take medication for my illnesses, on Christmas Eve, I took my first Fluoxetine. Shortly after Christmas, the issues in my relationship were mended, and I moved forward. I vowed to be a better partner by taking care of my mental health.

The following summer, I began my search for a horse that needed some extra miles or just one that I could ride on my own time and independent of the program I was riding in. I missed trail rides or schooling sessions with just me and my mount. I missed the connection that consistent day-in and day-out with the same horse formed.

My childhood coach reached out to me and asked if I was interested in training a horse that she had picked up from the barn where I was currently riding. I jumped at the opportunity to be back at the barn I considered home and where I could see Krissy every day.

I remember so vividly the first time I laid eyes on the cutest buckskin mare I had ever seen. Her eyes were soft, but her brows were furrowed with worry. She was quiet and gentle, and I immediately saw the appeal that my old coach had seen in her for her lesson program. This horse was clearly kind with a huge heart. There was something about her presence that put me at ease and eagerly made me agree to back and start her after spending only a few minutes observing her.

And here we are, to the place where my story converges with Mocha's into a story that cannot be separated.

Anyone other than a horse person will call me crazy for referring to this as love at first sight, but it certainly was a connection at first sight. However, those sweet eyes would soon show me that even the kindest horses have their issues.

Mocha was at the very bottom in a herd of twelve horses. I later learned that she had spent the first part of her life pastured with a sheep after another horse beat her up. At six years old, Mocha was turned out with other horses for the first time, and her quiet and shy demeanor did her no favors.

The next time I went out to catch Mocha in the field for our first ride, I was there for an hour while this horse ran laps around me as the others chased her away from me. Mocha was full of kick marks, cuts, bruises, and welts. A couple of months into our partnership, she was kicked in the head by the boss mare in her pasture and fractured her face, turning her into a real-life unicorn. Six years later, she still bears the lump, albeit smaller. Watching her in the pasture, it was clear that she did not have many horse friends.

By the winter, Mocha had begun to depend on me emotionally to the point that if she was in a barn full of people and horses, she would start trembling if I walked away from her. I cannot tell you why because she had only one owner before me, and she was in a very loving home. But for some reason, she was anxious whenever she was without me. My old coach observed this and kept an eye on Mocha when I returned to school during the week. It had become clear that Mocha was a one-person horse and would not be suitable for a lesson program.

I remember the phone call; it was a Thursday in March, and I was in a public policy lecture. When the call came through, I figured there was an emergency with Mocha, so I left the lecture hall to answer the phone. I was offered the option to purchase her. Otherwise, she would be advertised on the following Monday. Without hesitation, I said yes.

I was in my fifth year of university with one year left. I had no money, nowhere to keep her, and frankly, I had no business owning a horse, but I knew I was her person, and I could not send her with anyone else. When I considered her mental health, buying her was the only option. At the time, I was also in a year-long depressive episode, and I could not bear the thought of losing her. Like Krissy in my high school years, Mocha had become my coping mechanism on my bad days.

It turns out that not every horse can bear the emotional load that comes with their person's mental health. Krissy was the perfect example of a horse that set aside the emotional burden of their rider and focused on the task at hand. She was guarded emotionally from her history with humans that she did not trust, and therefore my bad days did not affect her. However, the first thing that my new coach told me about Mocha was that I could not even show

157

my face in the barn on a day that I was anxious.

Mocha was bonded to me emotionally, and her mental health depended on my mental health. This is significant because I was at a point in my life where anxiety attacks and panic attacks were a part of my every day. With big dreams of returning to the team penning arena, I had to change for this horse, otherwise training her would be difficult.

Once I bought Mocha, I had to move her to a full-service barn as I couldn't care for her while I was an hour away at school on weekdays. She went from a pasture with twelve horses to a paddock with just two others, an old Thoroughbred who was missing all of his teeth and a pony that was terrified of other horses. Mocha quickly befriended the pony—to the shock of the barn owners—and she stopped running from me in the pasture.

Despite the smaller pasture, the barn was chaotic. My rides were very unsuccessful. Mocha would spend our entire ride going full speed ahead in an outdoor ring with missing fence rails. I was genuinely afraid to ride her up there in fear she would run through the fence and leave the ring, out of control, with me on her.

With my mother's urging, I moved Mocha again—to the barn where she currently resides. With five other horses, big, clean stalls, and a barn family that began to understand Mocha's anxiety, I was able to create a chaos-free atmosphere for her to thrive. Running from me in the pasture became a once-in-a-while occurrence, and our issues were now solely under saddle.

Mocha was genuinely happy with her new living situation and her new friends. I learned that looking for a barn with an environment and standard of care suitable for me and my horse is worth the extra money. I knew this because I listened to my horse. Running away because of anxiety and fear is not normal. Being fearful of an otherwise gentle horse is not normal. Being in an environment where a kind and gentle soul turns dangerous, is not normal. From that day on, I promised Mocha I would listen to her.

That summer, my world collapsed when a relationship that I never thought would end ended. I was pitchpoled into the darkest depressive episode I had yet to experience. I found myself unable to be in a room alone without the onset of a panic attack. The rejection I felt left me feeling like I did not belong in this world and that I was not worthy of friendship or love. On my darkest days, it was the glimmer of that buckskin coat that lit the end of my dark tunnel.

I had a year-long journey in front of me until that depressive episode would end. When I went back for the final year of my master's program, to say it was a struggle would be a huge understatement. My friends brought up taking a year off from school multiple times in the first month after seeing just how bad my mental health was. I pushed them away and was determined to get it over with. I came home every weekend to be with my dog and Mocha because they were the only things that got me through the week.

To escape my depression, I decided to focus on Mocha's training. Our first issue was that she wouldn't walk while I was on her back. She had two speeds: out of control trot and gallop. The entire time I was on her back, her head was high, her body was rigid, and her ears did not stop moving. I knew she was anxious based on this body language, but I figured it was because being ridden wasn't something she was used to yet. This continued as I got her to walk, trot, canter, stop and steer. Once we had those basics down, I figured I could start her on cattle to make my dreams come true. Looking back, it was definitely too early, but I didn't know enough then.

We went to our first clinic about a year and a half after I had first backed her. That night I entered the warm-up late, which wasn't a bad thing as people fled the arena with their horses while Mocha ran uncontrollably. I was embarrassed and now anxious about how she would behave on cattle. The next day, she was the same in our morning warm-up, but to my surprise, she relaxed upon seeing the cattle. For the rest of the clinic, as long as the cattle were out, Mocha's anxiety lifted.

Freshly graduated from my master's, thanks to Mocha, and with a new career, I decided to start team penning that summer. It was the same. She was anxious and tense without cattle and more relaxed with them. My coach and I assumed that Mocha liked the cattle because her job became predictable, which eased her anxiety. We used that to develop a plan that I would ride consistently, do the same warm-up, and choose one thing to work on. Around the same time, my therapist suggested I also create a plan and stick to it to calm my anxiety. Within a week, I could get on her, and she would walk, something I struggled with for two years. It was clear that both of us needed to work on our anxiety. If not, we made a horrible team.

The next summer, I broke my leg playing rugby, which ended my twelve-year career in the sport and started my rough transition to retirement from someone who identified so strongly with their sport and as an athlete. One of my rugby teammates had grown up on a Quarter Horse ranch in Alberta and had mentioned that she missed riding. I told her she was more than welcome to try Mocha out, and she could ride her while I was injured.

Having another rider did not go over well for Mocha. After one ride, my friend agreed that for Mocha's mental health, it was probably best that she have a break while I was unable to ride. After two years under saddle, I realized that no one else would be able to ride my horse. This is where the give and take happens between horses and their riders; giving Mocha time off was what she needed for her mental health, even though I wanted her to continue being exercised.

The first month after I got back in the saddle, we had started to make great progress, thanks to the mental break that Mocha had also needed. A month later, Mocha had an accident in the trailer that resulted in a septic hock joint. For ten days, I listened to my veterinarian tell me that we weren't out of the woods yet in terms of possibly needing to euthanize. I spent hours in her stall crying, praying, and hoping that she would pull through. I wasn't sure how I would go on without her—I couldn't eat or sleep, and my anxiety worsened.

After the longest ten days of my life, we finally got a sample of joint fluid that was infection-free. She would still need to be on stall rest, and a chiropractor had to come in to fix her SI and hip, but Mocha would make it. The relief I felt was like nothing I had felt before.

After her accident, she began coming to me in the pasture with a nicker—a far cry from the horse that I used to spend an hour chasing around. I believe the vulnerability that I showed through my fear of losing her helped our relationship. She saw me as an empathetic guardian, afraid of losing her, rather than a source of anxiety.

With this newfound connection and my new coping mechanisms, when she returned to work, Mocha became softer under saddle. Her willingness to learn led to more saddle time because I finally felt like we were getting somewhere. I had spent three years frustrated that my horse continued to only be green broke. It turns out that we lacked an understanding of each other, leading to a breakdown in communication. It was not that she was a bad horse, nor that I was a bad trainer. It was that I was a bad communicator.

I was once a rider with a zero-tolerance and tough love type of attitude, but over time and with a lot of therapy, I learned to become more vulnerable and empathetic. I became softer in my thoughts toward myself and the others around me. Had it not been for Mocha's accident, I may have continued my tough façade, and Mocha may have never come to understand me, or me, her.

Once I felt I could take her off the property and not be ashamed of my "crazy" horse, I decided to take her to her first-ever roping clinic. It turns out we both showed potential in this new sport, and those at the clinic that had seen her before could not believe she was the same horse they once had to clear the arena for.

Mocha was the quietest horse of the bunch. In the warm-up, she moved softly off my legs, and while roping, she accepted the rope like an old pro— even when I roped her head by accident. After this clinic, we continued to rope all winter. I was over the moon with my horse. Rather than bringing her places and being embarrassed with what I had, I was confident and proud to show off my horse.

Cue the global pandemic of 2020.

It began to seem like whenever Mocha and I had some success, the world found a way to push us back down. Luckily, I was able to continue to ride my horse, and without anything else to do, I rode often. The social isolation created by the pandemic sent me into another downward spiral, and with Mocha as my only escape, she once again took the burden of my depression.

I immediately reached out to my therapist, knowing it was not fair for Mocha to deal with my emotions. In one of our sessions, she guided me through a meditation and had me imagine my perfect moment: It was on Mocha, galloping through the apple orchards that I grew up riding through. Every time I had a thought that my life wasn't worth it, I would close my eyes and imagine my perfect day with my golden girl. Each day with her was a blessing, and she gifted me with the feeling of pure happiness and fulfillment. I am sure that when I look at her with pride in my eyes, she feels it too.

But of course, the plot thickens. Just as horse events started opening up in the summer of 2020 in Nova Scotia, Mocha ended up three-legged lame the night before our first rodeo. With another visit from the vet, it was determined that Mocha had a muscle condition called fibrotic myopathy. My two options were retirement or surgery. I couldn't imagine not riding her again, but I also couldn't imagine a world where I could afford the surgery she needed. Luckily, I was pleasantly surprised by the cost of surgery. It turned out to be very affordable, so I shipped the golden girl two provinces away to the Atlantic Veterinary College.

When I took her off the trailer at the College, her head was high, and her brows were furrowed. She was anxious and easily startled as I handed her over to the surgical team that would be taking care of her. The Mocha I saw that day was the Mocha of years previous. Despite her visible anxiety, the team expressed how easy she was to work with. Surgery was a success, and Mocha would make a full recovery with an extensive rehabilitation program created by my veterinarian.

Now you would think that Mocha and I have the worst luck, which maybe we do. What you just read was the summation of a long five years with so many highs and lows—with accidents, bad luck, and mental health. But I can happily report that as of the summer of 2021, Mocha is sound, and we have started to rodeo.

The past year has seen the once "crazy" horse that cleared the area become a horse that people will go out of their way to ask her breeding, where she came from, and even compliment her. As I was packing up my ropes after a breakaway roping class at a local rodeo, the announcer came out of his booth to tell me that he really liked my horse and that you could see her heart and determination in her eyes the way she watched her calf, and in her body, as she waited (im)patiently for my cue.

He finished by saying, "She is going to be a really good rope horse." I am not sure that he will ever know just how happy he made me by giving a simple compliment without knowing the long road that brought us here, but as he walked away, my eyes welled up with tears, and I hugged my girl, beaming with pride.

The struggles that we faced together and the learning that we had to do taught me to listen to my horse, do what is best for her, and put judgment from others aside. These struggles were needed to address the shortcomings between us and forced me to learn how to cope effectively with my mental illnesses so that I could help Mocha deal with hers. Mocha knows a part of me that I'm not sure anyone else will, and because of that, she genuinely feels like a piece of my soul living outside of my body.

I once discussed how Mocha is not my type of horse with one of the practitioners that sees Mocha and my team penning mare, Sassy, quite frequently. I told her that Sassy, a fierce and independent, gritty mare, much like my old girl Krissy, is my type. I expressed that I thought it was funny that the horse I owned, and my heart horse, was not generally the type of horse I would select, but somehow, I couldn't pass her up.

Her response was, "That's because you didn't choose her. She chose you." Mocha gave me a little glance, and I started to tear up because I knew it was true.

My mental health was not ready for Mocha, but I needed her to heal and to turn myself into a softer and more understanding horsewoman and person in general. Because of Mocha, I am open to more perspectives, I judge less, and I have found happiness while living with my once crippling mental illnesses. Because of Mocha, I am kinder to myself and those around me. Because of Mocha, I am here.

I have had many people ask me why I don't just give her away and buy myself something of a higher caliber. Although Mocha may not be the most talented horse in the bunch, experiencing life with her is worth more than winning. She's my best friend, and I couldn't imagine going to a rodeo with another horse—plus she is turning into a neat little horse!

It took some extra time for her to mature mentally and physically and a surgery to fix her soundness issues. Just because a horse does not fit into the cookie-cutter mold of what others deem a horse should be, that does not mean they are not worthy of a try from us. Mocha has obliterated the box that we expect horses to fit into, and for that, I am thankful.

A million thank yous and I love yous will never be enough, my sweet, sweet Mocha.

About Brianna Graham

Brianna is from a rural farming village in Nova Scotia, Canada. She has always been drawn to animals, whether it be cattle, cats, dogs, or horses. She has been involved in the horse world for over two decades and now competes in team penning, sorting, and breakaway roping locally. In her time away from horses, she works in the agricultural policy field, plays hockey, and spends time with her border collie, Sabrina.

Brianna is an advocate for those with mental illness. For just under a decade, she has been a spokesperson for the Rugby Nova Scotia mental health campaign, "If you talk, I will listen." She attributes her healing and coping to the power that horses have for self-reflection, especially her anxious buckskin Mocha. Without horses and their healing powers, Brianna would not be in the place she is today.

Dedication

In loving memory of Duncan Graham.

To my grandfather, who was my link to the horse world and Mocha's biggest fan. He never tired of telling stories of his horses and border collie, even in his final days.

I will miss our post-horse show conversations, but I know you're racing through the lush fields of Inverness County in Heaven.

BOOK RECOMMENDATIONS

Take the Reins Podcast
*Everything is F*cked* by Mark Manson
A Journey to Softness by Mark Rashid

CHAPTER 15
TWO

BY DANIELLE SMALL

—

"Go pee!" I said to my dog, Peanut.

"Stay," I told her as she blocked my way out the door on my way to work. *This is unlike her.*

As I pulled out of the driveway and put on my favorite playlist: "Songs that make me want to sing along" Linda Ronstadt crooned over my car speakers. I started to sing along,

"I feel so ba . . . " but I could hear that the words weren't right. Strange. I loved this song. I knew every word. Skip it, I thought. *I feel like singing.* Except the same thing happened with every song. Songs I've sung my whole life. They sounded off.

The. Quick. Brown. Fox. Jumps. Over. The. Lazy. Dog.

Say it out loud. It's simple—unless you're having a stroke.

I managed "The quick . . . " and then the rest of the words are jumbled.

Not that I couldn't speak at all, it's wasn't baby talk. It was the wrong words in the wrong place.

I was having a stroke, and that's called aphasia.

Peanut had known.

I pulled up to a stop sign and moved my rearview mirror so I could see my face properly. I ran through other stroke risk factors. I smiled. *My face still works.* I raised both hands in the air. *Ok, I still have use of both sides of my body. Wow, I'm staying really calm.*

At this point, I decided to call my mom, not realizing that cars were starting to back up behind me on the rural road. I was suffering from both expressive aphasia and anomic aphasia. Expressive aphasia is frustrating. It's what I was experiencing in the car and on the phone with my mom. I knew what I wanted to say, but instead of thinking words, I thought more in feelings. I wanted to tell my mom, "Please meet me at the hospital. I'm having a stroke and am on my way there."

But the most I could get out was one word, "Help."

I wish I could say that the rest of the day passed in a blur. But I remember every terrifying moment. Calling my mom and hearing her panicking because she knows what a stroke sounds like because they run in our family.

Waving down traffic to help and knowing the people who stopped to help because, well, it is a small town. I remember hearing a woman I know comfort her kids between her yelling the words "chest pain" and our general location to the 911 operator.

Do I have chest pain? Nah, just a racing heart. I can still visualize the walk to the ambulance. I hate stretchers. I work in healthcare, so of course, I knew the paramedic, John. He talked to me, joked with me, and helped to keep me calm. Off we went.

The emergency room doctor was skeptical because they thought it was my heart. They hooked me to a heart monitor for most of the day, but in the end, I was sent home. "You need an MRI. Wait for the call. Take a day off work."

I knew that something was wrong with my brain when I looked down. Even my clothes looked off. I looked like a toddler dressed me. I knew that going home was wrong, but how was I to argue without sounding crazy?

Five days later, the MRI revealed that I had two strokes, one in the area of my brain that controls speech and language and the other in the back, the more mysterious part of our brains, where the memories are. The emergency room doctor called me personally to tell me, and he sounded sad on the phone.

The phone call was one of the more surreal moments of my life. I was sitting in the car with my mom. We had pulled over so that we didn't drive out of cell phone service. It was during that phone call that I found out that my life had just changed drastically. I was sitting on the side of the road, just meters from where I realized that I was having a stroke in the first place. I had put the doctor on speakerphone because I wanted my mom to be able to hear things firsthand rather than having to relay the information when it was fresh, and I am glad I did.

I was twenty-nine years old at the time of my strokes. When you have a stroke, especially when you are young, you are assigned a stroke coordinator. My stroke coordinator was a literal woman warrior. She was an entire support system in the body of one woman. I met with her about seven days after my stroke. One of the things we did together was take the time to literally pick through every aspect of my life to look for risk factors.

I never expected to feel so vulnerable in a room. She planned and took care of things for me. She was exactly what I needed her to be at a time when my brain felt it had blank spaces where my life should be.

My speech was not back to where it needed to be, so speaking was frustrating. Since my early twenties, I had worked in healthcare as a pharmacy practice assistant, so I was used to seeing patients and their families just hours after a crisis. When I was sitting in the stroke coordinator's office, I wondered if my face looked like that of my patients? *Did I look hollow? Like I was frozen, not in fear, but just frozen with a numb look on my face?* I wondered, but I didn't really want to know. I left the hospital exhausted. This was going to be a long road.

Throughout my stroke journey, I recognized the look on my mom's face. I had seen that look before at work. She looked tired and worried. But she also looked so helplessly uncertain.

The speech came back slowly. That is the anomic aphasia. I struggled to find the right words for things that I wanted to say. I had my strokes on December 4th, so I wanted to attend family functions over the holiday season. I practiced obsessively, going over typical conversations that I ran into daily. My stroke coordinator recommended that I talk to a therapist.

Reluctantly, I booked a session. We discussed the big things, school, work, what I felt other people expected of me, and a shiny new Obsessive-Compulsive Disorder diagnosis. I didn't notice the impact the stroke had on my memories right away. The speech was concerning since it was most obvious.

The memory loss almost crept up on me. *I'm supposed to be doing my master's in sociology. I know my topic, but what was my point?* My research was unfamiliar. *Who was I when I wrote that? I sound smart. Can I still do that?* So many questions. So much upheaval. Nothing felt quite like home. Nothing felt right.

My house was wrong, my job was wrong, my thesis was wrong. Driving felt worse than ever—the OCD hates driving. The words are wrong. And the horse was wrong.

I bought Duke when I was twenty-one years old. He was an untouched stallion who called to me from across the world, literally. I spent eight months in Australia, surrounded by incredible warmbloods, and couldn't stop thinking about the feral golden stallion I had met back in small-town Nova Scotia. When I came home, I bought him immediately. He was almost completely untouched. He would accept a halter but didn't lead, and I could brush him, as long as I didn't want to touch anywhere other than his shoulder.

He was the very definition of a project horse. We grew up together: halter breaking, heartbreaks, learning to pick up his feet, and finding my own in my career. He also saw me through a Rheumatoid Arthritis diagnosis in my early twenties. My body betrayed me, and the medications that I was prescribed battered my confidence and my strength. I was suddenly unable to ride through behaviors that would have made me laugh just months before.

Duke and I compromised. He was mostly too much for me to ride with my RA, but we connected through liberty work, so I took clinics with respected trainers in my area. We could dance, and that was more than enough then.

When I finally found a medication that managed my arthritis, I wanted to ride again, and I wanted to catch up on things I felt I had missed. Not to compete, but to spend my time exploring, trail riding, and enjoying the saddle. Duke had other ideas. We clashed but kept trying. During one of our clashes, I fell off and broke my ankle in three places.

Surgery. Steroids. Bed rest. Sedentary lifestyle.

Being sedentary is a huge risk factor for a stroke.

It's a stretch, but I feared him, and in a lot of ways, I blamed him for my stroke. . . but most of all, I loved him. When I shut my eyes and ran my hands across his back in a quiet moment, I knew every inch. I didn't forget the feel of him under my hands. But we were no longer right for one another. If I'm honest with myself, he hadn't been right for me for a long time.

Trusted trainers and friends had gentle conversations with me for years, suggesting that I find a horse better suited to my needs. My physical limitations had strained our relationship from the beginning. Duke is a horse that needed someone dedicated to him. He needed continuous and consistent work. When my RA set in, this was just not something that I could do with him. And once I broke my ankle, it felt like we were never going to be on the same page. He deserved someone without the baggage, and honestly, so did I.

I set Duke up well. I loved him deeply, even though he was no longer right for me. I hired a trainer I respected to give him a couple of months of training, and I listed him at a fair price. I had a huge response to the advertisement. Several interested parties reached out, but the situation wasn't ideal until a young woman contacted me, and I knew she was the one.

I wanted her to want him, which was a weird feeling. I watched her mount up and ride off. Perfect. I won't buy a horse until next spring, I thought as Duke left in a trailer. I was not crying, and I felt so proud that I had made the right decision for both of us. I knew that my decision was right. *She is perfect. He'll be good.*

I browsed obsessively for horses. *I'm not looking, but if the right one comes up, I'll buy it.* That was a lie I told myself sagely.

A call from a friend declaring that she has found the one changed things very quickly for me. "She is an Arabian cross." Those were magic words. I loved Arabian horses. My mom had a barn full, so what was one more? Her name was Lia, and she was green broke—but that wasn't what I wanted. I promised myself a safe, broke, quiet horse that I could trail ride right away. *Whatever! Let's just go look. We're not committed to anything.*

She was lovely, naturally. I could tell she was kind right away. They told me she'd never had consistent work. However, they told me this after I had ridden her, in a nice frame, as if she was well broke. She was so willing; I wouldn't have pushed like that if I knew her training lacked consistency. The next thing I knew, we were doing a vet check for her, and she was mine—six months earlier than intended.

Lia was, and is, not perfect. It is unfair to put such a label on a living thing. No, she wasn't perfect, and the timing was not ideal. Still, she turned out to be exactly what I needed. Her previous owners didn't ask much of her, and she was kept as a companion horse, so we took a step back. We long-lined, I taught her to respond to pressure, but most importantly, I rode.

I took a few lessons from the barn owner at my boarding stable who knew my story. He knew where I was and why I was scared. Lia was kind, and that was what mattered. It took less than three groundwork sessions to have her standing like a statue while I mounted up.

Along with the stroke, the OCD took away my love of learning for a long time. I had signed myself up for clinics with trainers that I had worked with for years, but I canceled them, even though I was physically able after my stroke. I felt embarrassed, and I didn't want those people to hear me struggle with my speech. I also didn't want them to know that I didn't remember things we had worked on in the past.

I spoke extensively with my therapist about how people perceived me. I was very concerned about what people expected me to be. I defined myself as someone intelligent and educated. The fact that I constantly pursued knowledge and learned almost effortlessly was something that I once relished. But after the strokes, I stopped learning, left my master's program, canceled clinics, and stopped reading. I had always been an avid reader of fiction, non-fiction, and theory. I loved political theory as well as the theory of horsemanship.

By sheltering myself away from education and holding back my own horsemanship journey, I prevented some of my own healing. By being afraid of putting myself back out there, I was unconsciously presenting that I was still "sick." I noticed that people were treating me differently. Their expectations lowered. The thing is, unlike people, horses don't lower their expectations.

My strokes happened in December of 2019. I sold Duke in the summer of 2020 and bought Lia a month later. My real progress with Lia didn't start until the spring of 2021. It is fascinating how many things can change with two strokes and two horses within two years. Until very recently, I would have told you that I used Lia as therapy. I used her to heal what my health had broken.

I moved Lia from a boarding facility back to my mom's hobby farm. My mom and I began collaborating on her training. Horses have always been how my mother and I have bonded and spent time together. I also started working with a new trainer—a fresh start.

Ada Draghici understood my health limitations, and in a recent training session, she said something that stuck with me. She said that she dislikes hearing people say that their horse is their therapist. Ada believes that it is up to us, the trainer or rider, to meet the horse where they are on that particular day. This resonated with me deeply.

After my strokes, I fell into a rut. I started to make excuses for myself. Purchasing Lia changed the game. To move forward with Lia, I needed to start showing up. Not just showing up physically and putting in the time, I needed to commit real brainpower. This was *not* easy.

I was not immediately able to commit to long training sessions. I needed to retrain my brain to concentrate for longer periods of time.

Ada allowed me to audit her lessons with a friend to start relearning old skills and exposing me to some new ones. Breaking down the barriers that I had erected took some time. I worried a lot in the beginning that I was not going to develop a deep relationship with Lia, but now that I have worked through opening up to her, I realize that *I* was blocking that relationship, not *her*.

I originally stated that I wanted to buy a finished horse when I sold Duke. While I think that I would have enjoyed buying a well-trained horse, I think that buying Lia was a fantastic choice. I have the necessary skills to train a green horse and am willing to accept help when it is offered or needed, but, most importantly, it has allowed me to access memories, and practice skills that I worried were lost forever.

I started to read again, and I also began to write in a journal. I have never been one to journal. I'm not sure if it is a matter of a dislike of serious introspection or simply not taking the time for myself. However, I began a training journal to record my work with Lia. This was frustrating at first. I could picture my training session in my head but getting it down on paper was challenging.

Looking back on the first few entries in my notebook can be emotional for me. The thoughts don't flow; my word choice is erratic; my handwriting is atrocious; and my spelling is questionable at best. The perfectionist in me sometimes prevents me from journaling.

I don't have time or the energy to write anything worth reading. What is the point? It's been so long since I've written. Why start again now? But having Lia to write about has kept me on track, and the simple act of writing has helped to improve my writing skills for work and other areas of my life.

I have often found it a bit annoying when people say that major traumatic events in their lives changed them for the better. I think, Wow, you've just had your world rocked, and you think you're now living your best life? So, I won't tell you that my stroke was good for me, but I will tell you that it was clarifying. My physicians and stroke team have not been able to find the cause of my stroke at this time, so I don't have any specific instructions on how to prevent another one. I take a blood thinner, but other than that, I'm still in the dark.

To keep myself from going crazy with worry, I took a look at risk factors and adjusted my life to avoid as many as I can. I made a commitment to move my body more every day. This does not mean vigorous exercise. Being chronically ill, it's just not in the cards every day. Sometimes moving my body is as simple as making sure I am home, cook my meals, and look after my horse.

As I mentioned earlier, it is easy to let myself down, but I need to hold myself accountable to Lia.

About Danielle Small

Danielle is a lifelong equestrian from the beautiful Annapolis Valley, Nova Scotia, where she lives with her dog, Peanut. Danielle attended Acadia University and currently works as a Coordinator for Nova Scotia Health. Danielle is not a competitive equestrian; however, she strives to make her horses as exceptional as possible with continued lessons and training centered primarily around dressage.

Dedication

To all the equines that came before, to my family, and to my found family, thank you for helping to put the pieces back together—then and now.

Book Recommendations

Ada Draghici Relationship-Based Horsemanship (Facebook page)
Sitting Horse Tribe www.sittinghorse.us with Farrah Green (Membership to the tribe includes access to massive video library and weekly Q & A with Farrah).

Horse Woman: Notes on Living Well & Riding Better by Lee McLean (Canadian content!)

CHAPTER 16
MURPHY'S LAW REWRITTEN
BY KATHLEEN ARROWSMITH

———

"Honor the unseen hours. It's how I try to remember that what I'm admiring in other people took days and sometimes decades to get right. And I think about that a lot when things get hard."

– Chelsea Yamase

THE DAY MURPHY was born, it must have been quite a sight. Gangly long legs, a blackish coat that would eventually turn red-brown, and ears. Huge ears. So big that someone thought the name "Donkey" would suit him. No, it couldn't be Donkey, but the movie *Shrek* was coming out, and Eddie Murphy played a character named Donkey. Thus, Murphy became his name. Life began. Fortunately, and perhaps a tad surprisingly, he grew into the ears and the legs. His coat turned liver chestnut interrupted by a wide blaze and hind stockings.

Murphy grew up in the northern United States and, as a youngster, he was shown successfully in leadline classes. Early on, it became apparent that he was a sensitive horse—it didn't take much to evoke his sympathetic nervous system: fight or flight. Most of his first few years of life is a mystery to those who know him now. Indeed, his story truly started when he met Judi.

176

Judi bought Murphy as a four-year-old intending to make him her next dressage horse. She was close to retirement and knew the Quarter Horse breed had a reputation for being sensible and reliable. Unfortunately, Murphy quickly revealed himself to be altogether opposite from the stereotype.

When Judi brought Murphy home, she soon discovered he was a nervous wreck. He spooked at birds, at people, at nothing. He would bolt and buck until his rider came off. He would scramble madly and rear on the cross ties until they snapped, and he could run. His confidence was in shambles and his trust in humans was non-existent. Judi battled both her own fears and his for years. She suffered countless injuries from riding Murphy, but she continued to make the courageous decision to come back the next day, try again, and keep the horse.

Several horse trainers tried their hand at fixing Murphy. He spent time at a trainer's where he was so uncontrollable that he broke three pairs of reins and afterward was ridden in nylon lead ropes. He was excused from clinics, given up on by coaches, and had everyone in his life unsure of what to do next. He was unpredictable, terrified, and, most of all, dangerous.

I met nine-year-old Murphy when I was fifteen, after he'd caused an accident that involved broken bones, a severe concussion, and emotional trauma for everyone involved. He had spooked, bolted, and bucked until his rider had fallen off and sustained serious injuries. Worse, it wasn't the first time.

This was the last straw.

Judi made the astonishingly brave choice so many wouldn't have made. She chose not to sell Murphy. Instead, she searched for help. Many trainers said no to taking him on. He was too far gone, too dangerous—a feral thing with no hope of becoming a willing partner.

In many ways, his trip to Dan Northrup's barn was his last chance. Fortunately, the moment he walked into the barn, he started on a new path that would lead toward a future no one likely ever thought possible. He spent six months in training with Dan and came out a changed animal.

Dan started over entirely with Murphy, giving him the opportunity to progress through his anxiety. Dan treated him as if he wasn't the creature who had caused so many injuries. Rather, Murphy was just another horse there to be educated. It was exactly what Murphy needed.

Dan gave Murphy a chance. In truth, he probably saved his life. After those six months, it was as if someone had hit the reset button on Murphy. The bucking was gone. Instead of bolting, he would just tense. When he was unsure of what to do, his default was to put his head down and back up. Murphy had come far from the horse, wild with fear, that he once was. He was no longer quite so broken, but he also wasn't whole yet. Murphy had a lot of healing left to do, the kind that takes years of patience, thousands of hours, and dirt ground so far into your hands that you think they may never scrub clean.

Compared to some, I was a late-comer to the equestrian sport, not starting to take lessons until my mid-teens. As a beginner, I was lumped in with others of my skill level—elementary school-aged kids. While I found that horrifyingly embarrassing, it really didn't matter. I was hooked. I spent every second I could at the barn, cleaning stalls, feeding horses, and leading them to and from the pasture. I would do anything to be near the giants that I had learned to love so much. The people that I met at the barn would become my closest friends: human and horse.

I was certainly not a naturally gifted rider. I struggled endlessly with my position and sitting the gaits. I didn't advance as quickly as I should have through the lesson program, and I was forever grateful for the patience my coach showed me.

I remember the day I got to ride Murphy for the first time. I was thrilled. He wasn't my usual lesson pony, but I knew him from doing the afternoon chores, and he'd quickly become my favorite to lead in, feed, and be around. We just seemed to *get* each other. He knew what I would do before I did it. We were in sync in the right ways. This feeling transferred to under saddle, and we had a phenomenal lesson.

Soon after that first lesson, I was asked if I'd like to lease Murphy. He'd been out of training for months at this point and was beginning to revert to his old ways. He needed to continue to evolve instead of regress, and his owner was in search of a young rider to help control his energy level. My coach hoped it would be a good match. It certainly wasn't because of my talent that they had chosen me. I had little of that, but I was there nearly seven days a week doing barn chores, and that dedication had shone through.

It has been almost a decade since then, and everything has changed since the first time I stepped into Murphy's stall.

In less than a year, my life had morphed from horseless to days that looked like this: school, barn chores, time with Murphy, then home to do schoolwork until I fell asleep. As time passed and I found myself in the twelfth grade, my passion for animals only grew, and I also worked at my local veterinary clinic.

Murphy has always been and continues to be a difficult horse. Combined with my inexperience, we were often just shy of disaster in our early days. And yet I was there every day, spending hours riding, or lunging, or just being with him. He quickly became my best friend through the frigid winter days and long nights, muddy boots, calloused palms, sweat, and tears. We spent not hundreds but thousands of hours together. I didn't always know what I was doing. I still don't. I just knew that I loved this animal more than any I had ever been around.

We got better together, and Murphy learned that he could trust me. Humans weren't all bad, and many have had a hand in his transformation. Early on, I learned as much from my friends as any coach. Connecting with this group of horse people and immersed alongside them daily, I found myself copying their movements and taking advantage of their endless patience to answer my questions.

Murphy and I have been fortunate to take lessons and clinics in many disciplines over the years: trail, western pleasure, hunter under saddle, and the list goes on. Our favorites, though, were the few liberty clinics we did. It added new meaning to the work that we'd been doing off-line.

I spent hours learning to read him and for him to learn to read me. He knew that when I picked up my energy it was his cue to canter, and I knew that when he got an extra wrinkle above his eye that he was worried. I discovered when a pat on the neck would reassure him, and he realized that he could look to me for guidance when he got stressed. In every gesture, I told him "I am here; I am yours"—a subtle language, invisible to onlookers.

I've never believed in the popular idea of "heart horses." I think that if you spend enough time to really understand them, to love them, any horse will find their way into your heart. But perhaps I believe that because I've already

179

found the horse that has mine.

Murphy had always been at the bottom of the pecking order in his herd, bullied and pushed out of the way by his pasture mates. Over time, through our work, he developed newfound confidence that he carried with him everywhere he went. The other horses sensed this and started to respect him. He grew into a leader.

Murphy became the go-to horse for ponying colts under saddle and teaching them manners out in the pasture. I've learned from Murphy that the things we teach our horses have more power than we know. We can give them tools to use apart from us that can change their lives.

Over time, and almost imperceptibly, Murphy began to change. He ceased to spook at all, sighing in contentment when humans approached instead of flapping his lower lip with anxiety. It felt like we were finally hitting our stride. Murphy and I excelled in our liberty work, earning a spot of recognition for it around the barn. I was excited every day to watch videos online and figure out what we could learn next.

I could let him off lead in the field outside, and he would stay with me—no tack, no ropes, no fences containing him. He would stay. I could warm him up off lead in a pen full of show horses and take him off the property with no worry about his old anxiety returning. He received a lot of interesting looks as I led him around the showgrounds with just a simple loop around his neck. I rode him bareback and bridleless, took him on solo trail rides, and gave him my total trust. The best place in the world was by his side.

Looking back now, those days were golden. Even when it rained, the sun shone on Murphy. It's not that we have never been discouraged. Some days I feel as if I'm just starting to figure out the horse training thing, only to have a day go so wrong that I wonder if I deserve to ever be around them again. I've been bruised and bled, hit the ground, and had any sense of pride beaten into humility. I've been hurt by horses, by my own mistakes. However, I am fortunate to have friends who dust me off and call it *experience*.

Murphy has hurt me, but I've hurt him, too. I've asked him for too much, too fast, too soon. I've made him sore; I've made him stressed. Each time it happened, it has made one thing very clear: There is no worse pain than hurting the one you love most.

But the sun would rise the next day, and I would return to the barn to be reminded why I love horses so much.

As Murphy and I started to progress with liberty training, I began getting requests for people to try it with him. I was eager to show off what he had learned and how far he had come, so I agreed. I was shocked when he refused to stay with them. He would play along for a minute or two, and then he would run away to stand distanced from them.

I wondered why, but then I realized he didn't stay with me just because I'd trained him to. The others didn't speak Murphy's language as I did, and when he sent signals that he was worried, or tired, or uninterested, they didn't see them. So the connection to them broke, and he left.

The truth is, animals see you for who you truly are. There are no lies. At liberty, when the connection is weak, Murphy will leave. When he does, I know he will always come back, but he has also made it clear that I've done something wrong and left no room for ego as he goes. This is the hidden treasure of horses—the ebb and flow of true connection.

It was years before Murphy developed enough tolerance that he would stay with strangers. If I passed him on to a new person, leadership transferred by a pat on the neck, he was assured that I trusted them already, and he would be okay. He had the tools to deal with his insecurities on his own without constant support from me.

Along the way, I decided I wanted to teach Murphy to lie down on cue. There are many ways to do this, the most common being to use ropes to hobble the horse, so they have no choice but to lie down. While this method has its place and is certainly the best fit for most wanting to teach this, I knew immediately it wasn't right for Murphy. He'd spent so long carrying the baggage of mistrusting humans, and my real goal had nothing to do with him lying down.

I wanted to give Murphy the power to be vulnerable. To teach him that he could have the courage to willingly put himself in a defenseless position and that no humans would hurt him. What I didn't know was that it would be the greatest test of patience I'd ever had. I taught him to get round and soft when I tapped his belly and relax downwards. It was three years of work before he learned to do this, and I knew then that we had broken through the last of his trust issues. He knew that he could be entirely trusting of humans, and everything would be okay. No one would hurt him as they must have done all those years ago.

It nearly became a tradition for each newcomer to the barn to get a little demonstration from Murphy and me, as well as a brief history of his past. I would give him to them at liberty, and then I would talk them through asking for each of his skills. He would do liberty circles for them, fetch their glove, bow down on one knee, and back up when they picked up his tail. No ropes or fences were binding him. His ability to please the crowd became a skill of its own.

Over the years, I've been told by some of the people introduced to Murphy that they wish they could "have a horse just like Murphy." I think that's when I know how immense his transformation has been. They can't see any remnants of the terrified animal he once was. They don't know that having a horse like him has involved countless hours and nearly a decade of work.

It has always been about the horse for me. The riding, the liberty, and the tricks were never my first love. It has always been about him—about our connection, about understanding another on a level that transcends words and spans between species. The times that I've been the happiest are by his side or on his back. We have lived our lives in the arena, and I have grown up in his company. He may know me better than any human could.

From the highest heights, we find our lowest lows. I graduated high school and spent two years working toward my bachelor's degree at the local university. I told people it was to save money, but I couldn't bear to leave Murphy. I'm happy that I stayed. It was in those years that we made a large part of our progression.

I was thrilled to be accepted into the Doctor of Veterinary Medicine class of 2022 at the Atlantic Veterinary College. Leaving for vet school should have been a celebration. Instead, I dreaded it. Many nights alone at the barn, I would sit in the arena dirt, Murphy's nose in my hair, and breath on my cheek. He didn't know I was leaving, but he *knew*. I didn't know how I would go without Murphy.

Loving him has been the best and the worst parts of my life. I love him more than anything on the planet, but he isn't mine, and so my heart is not my own.

I've never been a particularly emotional person. I'm overly logical, and training as a veterinarian has only accentuated that part of me and drowned out most of what could be considered *feelings*. Without fail, though, speaking of Murphy draws tears to my eyes and a tremor to my voice. Since I've been gone for school, it has been asked if others should take my place by his side and by Judi's.

Such simple questions never fail to summon the tears. I fear losing him to someone else; I fear that he might not be treated as I think he should; I fear that he'll turn back into that terrified version of himself that will always be a possibility. Selfishly, most of all, I fear that someone else will be better with him and that he will grow to love them more.

At times, it feels that I'm not enough. Like I'll never be good enough to deserve him, no matter who we impress by his training or what degree I prove myself worthy of. It takes clawing myself out of that hole to realize that I've always been enough for Murphy. He doesn't understand the semantics of these things, and he wouldn't care if he could. He is connected to me in the same way that I am to him, and for him, that is enough. It always has been.

Over the years, I've learned to bite my tongue and hide a broken heart when a decision is made that I don't agree with. I've wondered before if the heartache is worth it. And, of course, it is: The price of loving an animal so greatly is always worth the risk of losing it all.

That's horses, isn't it? We trade moments of pain and sadness for ones of harmony, happiness, and of belonging. They force us to be present and to look within.

I've been blessed that somewhere along the way, Judi began calling him "our" horse. I don't think she realizes the magnitude of this simple kindness. She has told me before that she maybe would not have been able to keep him if not for the hours I spent as a teen all those years ago, and, whether or not this is true, it is a flattery that warms me.

I've learned countless lessons from the barn that carried me through my teenage years and continue to serve me on the rocky path into adulthood. For the most part, these aren't lessons that anyone can teach. They're lessons learned from hours spent with a broom or a lead rope in my hand, from a horse by my side, and from good people around me. I learned to always help where you can, even if it goes unnoticed, to tell the people and animals in your life how amazing they are every day, to know that some family is chosen, and Judi is as much family as my own blood. She means more to me than she may ever know.

Murphy has done liberty in warm-up rings full of other horses, laid down on cue in the middle of lessons, and became what once seemed impossible. People who knew Murphy before don't recognize him now. I suppose they may not recognize me either. He is so, so loved by everyone he meets.

I am who I am today because of him. I owe so much to that big brown horse. I can only hope that he cares for me a fraction as much as I love him. Murphy is my whole heart, and he is home.

Always.

About Kathleen Arrowsmith

———

Kathleen is a self-proclaimed horse and animal lover—a lover of anything four-legged, with a passion for animal training and behavior. Kathleen is a proud graduate of the Doctor of Veterinary Medicine class of 2022 at the Atlantic Veterinary College. She is looking forward to a wonderful animal-filled career as a veterinarian. She has been privileged to be able to help other people and horses in their journeys as she continues learning on her own. In her spare time, when she's not at the barn with Murphy, Kathleen enjoys photography, hiking, and spending time with her cat, Dove and rabbit, Dragon.

Dedication

To Judi, for facing life with strength and courage.

Book Recommendations

The Scorpio Races by Maggie Stiefvater
How Stella Learned to Talk by Christina Hunger

CHAPTER 17
UP IN FLAMES
BY NIKKI PORTER

——

"SIT DOWN AND be quiet like the good girl you used to be."
These words were spoken sharply by a family member. She would rather I sat silently at her table drinking tea, pretending to be okay, than have an open and vulnerable conversation in an attempt to address problems in our relationship and family that had gone ignored for far too long.

I was in my late twenties, and my emotions had come to a boiling point after years of pain, confusion, and hurt. Instead of being met with compassion, I was met with a stern look and a calculated voice—a brick wall. I was silenced. My knees were taken out from under me by those thirteen words strung together into the most dismissive sentence I had ever heard.

I sat down; I shut up; and I never sat at that table again. I can thank being an equestrian, and three particular ponies, for the strength to do so.

I grew up as the youngest in the house for most of my childhood life; that only changed when I was thirteen and my younger sister was born. When I was little, I was patient because I had to be, and I was quiet because I knew someone was always there, even if it took some time for them to get to me. I was an equalizer from the very start of my life. I didn't like to make waves, and I quickly sprang into action to smooth out any waves I saw being created by my siblings, cousins, or friends. I liked peace and calm, and I have worked to create it since I can remember. I am a rule follower through and through.

Even now, at the age of thirty-seven, if I feel like I may be breaking a rule, not even a law, I get a sick feeling in my stomach. It is one of the only things that I find difficult to self-regulate and parent myself through, even after years of dedicating my time and energy to finding ease within myself in a world filled with stress and chaos.

My need to feel peace and calm has never left me, but my methods to create it have changed dramatically. In the past, I desperately tried to change what was happening around me, and I used to shrink and make myself small to avoid adding to the noise—so others would be happy—and I wouldn't feel like I, or anyone else, would get into trouble.

Now, I do my best to worry less about fixing the environment to the detriment of showing up as my authentic self and, instead, I make sure I am the source of my own calm. I owe the skills to do so, to the horses who I have been privileged to own, ride, and care for over the last thirty-two years. I now see how the need to create peace from such a young age translated into a desire to become a teacher and then how it caused me to leave my teaching career nine years down the road. My life has been shaped by my need to influence my environment and the people in it so I can be more at ease in myself.

Who would have guessed being told to sit and be quiet like a "good girl" would be the catalyst that enabled me to find my voice? I now stand strong in my personal and professional beliefs and choose to live life according to my values and what brings me joy, versus what others think I should say or do. Those words ignited the fire, but the lessons taught to me as an equestrian are the foundation that allowed me to believe in myself, to level up and to follow my heart despite the flames.

"Arabian pony." That may be all I have to say for you to understand the best and worst idea my parents ever had when they decided to get us into horses. I was taught grit early on in my horse career. My first pony was a gray Arabian/

Welsh mare with a strong personality and sense of self-preservation.

Her name was Ripple, and she taught me grit like no other. I shared Ripple with my older sister, Lisa, and she taught us her lessons equally to both of us. Neither of us left our time with Ripple the same kids we were when my parents unloaded her from the trailer her first day with us on a crisp fall day in 1990. She was our family's first horse, and she was the perfect amount of fun and furry to make us ask for help and allow us to experience the joy and magic made between horses and kids.

When I was seven years old, my grandfather told me something that stuck with me for life. He said that "It takes someone falling off one hundred times before they are a true rider." Either Ripple heard this and made it her mission to have me claim the title of rider, or—the more likely case—my grandfather saw the possibility of every fall snuffing the passion to be an equestrian, out of a young girl's heart.

Ripple quickly acquainted me with the ground and another old saying, "If you fall off, get right back on." I wanted to try everything from jumping to racing, and I fell off trying it all. Falling off started to become a part of riding for me. I knew when I hit the ground to lay still and to catch my breath before I attempted to get up, and when I got back up, I always got back on.

Grit is a personality trait possessed by someone who has passion and perseverance. When my grandfather told me it took one hundred falls to be a true rider, I believe it was his way of saying that equestrians have grit and our horses are the ultimate teacher. Without Ripple's valuable lessons at such an early stage in my horse career, I likely would not have had what it took in the future to do the work needed to reach the goals I created both in and out of the arena.

I have learned that choosing to honor yourself, find your voice, and make the commitment to use it while living a life driven by self-belief, is the most rewarding thing a person can do. I have also learned that in doing that comes tests that eventually led to clarity, to the lessons my horses have taught me along the way. Doing what is best for you doesn't always feel like freedom. Sometimes it feels like holding a match that burns itself out and making the connection—seeing that you are burning down things you know and have grown to love.

In my efforts to live a life I was proud to call my own and address the parts of myself that were holding me back from doing so, I didn't intend to burn anything down. However, I discovered that some things surrounding me were incredibly flammable and went up in flames as soon as the match was lit. Not everything went up in smoke. The relationships, values, and opportunities that had solid foundations were strengthened by my growth, and love remained. Some, I dare say became stronger as a result. Other things that lacked depth and substance burned on their own time.

As I assessed my life—my decisions, my actions, my commitments, and my relationships—I could feel the heat building around the things that did not align with who I truly was. I was so determined to uncover more of who I was with every book I read, course I enrolled in, every risk I took, boundary I set, and change I made. There have been many days I felt like the smoke from all the things I seemed to set on fire would choke me to death.

In the beginning, I would put my head in my hands and cry until the smoke cleared and I could see and breathe again. Now, I find myself mustering the strength and resolve to keep walking in the direction I was going before the fire started. The smoke engulfs me, and I find my way to fresh air rather than waiting helplessly for the winds to change and clear it away for me. It still burns my eyes and takes my breath away, but it won't stop me from moving forward, toward becoming the best and most authentic person I can be. And along the way, learning more about the people I care about and how to express my understandings of events in a way that validates them—and how we know each other in positive ways. And to leave the rest in the dust behind me. Wanting those of like mind, of learners together, to move forward in a direction that strengthens and affirms us all.

I remember a day, a few years back, that I witnessed a friendship burn right before my eyes that I thought was made of stone. She was put in an awkward position of being friends with me still after some mutual friendships had shifted apart. I remember overhearing a conversation that revealed that she had lied to me to avoid me hurting me. It made me sad to think she thought I would be mad or upset, so I decided to address it with her. I walked directly to her and told her what I had heard. I told her sincerely as I pulled her in for a hug that she did not ever need to lie to me, especially about that. I hugged her with a loving intention and genuine understanding of the position she was in.

What I learned in the arena that day was that people hear and see us based on who they need or want us to be, not who we are. She did not feel my love and compassion. She heard the words, "Don't lie to me." Our friendship went up in flames at that moment. I felt it, and it broke my heart because I knew that she no longer saw me for who I was. She was seeing me for who she heard others say I was, others who needed to not like me for their own worlds to make sense.

It was months later when I sat in the passenger seat of a mutual friend's car and cried until my body was weak and my eyes were swollen that I began to understand that her behavior was not about me. I felt like I was surrounded by a wildfire and lost something I could not replace as a result of a gust of wind. I had come to terms with some friendships that had turned to ash over the years of change and growth, knowing it was what was best for both them and me, but the ones that were unexpected hurt more than I was ready for.

That lost friendship was not the only one I cried over, but it set a precedent for the pain I would feel and the way I knew I needed to work through it. I learned that I had to keep walking while the fire was burning to prevent long-term scars. It was also important to sit with and feel the effects when it was safe to do so. I discovered that no matter how old I got, the safest place to truly feel my emotions, be myself, and show up fully, was in the barn. It is in the barn that I have grieved the loss of friendships, family members—four and two-legged, jobs, beliefs, hopes, dreams, and parts of myself.

After walking through another fire recently, I was reminded of the grit instilled in me by Ripple so many years ago. Amid some heavy emotions, the feelings of passion and perseverance were tangible as I remained true to myself, my worth, and my vision for my future. I could see the test for what it was, and I was able to use the lessons I had learned to pass it. With every fall off Ripple's back, I felt like I was one step closer to becoming something rather than feeling like I was *failing* at something. As an adult navigating the challenges of growth, change, and loss, I feel that familiar feeling of *becoming*, which stops me from quitting.

I was nine and knew that the ponies always came first on Christmas morning. My sister and I scrambled to get on our warm clothes so we could quickly feed and get back to the house for presents and breakfast. With the guise of feeding the horses their treats from their stockings, my parents, and my nanny and papa, who lived with us, all headed to the barn together. Our barn had sliding wooden doors with bars on the front and on that morning, there was a stocking on each stall that housed a horse.

This Christmas morning, it was brought to my attention that "Santa" had left an extra stocking on a stall that normally sat empty. They told me to go over and grab the treats, knowing what I would see, and that was the moment I experienced what every young horse girl's dreams are made of.

Looking at me through the bars was Little Smokey, a black, fuzzy, chubby pony with a perfect half-moon on his forehead. I didn't know it then, but that was the first day of rebuilding the confidence Ripple had taken out of me on her mission to teach me grit. Smokey was the opposite of Ripple in all the ways, right down to his color. He was the best Christmas present—other than my engagement ring from Mike many years later—that I have ever received. We would spend the next four years doing brave things together with the support of my parents and riding coach. He taught me confidence and courage.

Smokey took me through my entry levels of Pony Club, introduced me to the hunter world, eventing, and that the need for trust is the foundation of both confidence and courage with our horses and in life. He taught me that half the battle was to trust him, and the other half was to trust myself. Smokey was the first horse I owned to show me that humans could rob an animal of the thing they need most for their survival, a sense of safety. It was as though in his teaching me how to trust, he was reminding himself as well. I began riding strong and knew I *could* stay on rather than getting on despite the fear of the *fall*.

Confidence and courage are the by-products of trust. I owe my willingness to trust again after being hurt, to Smokey. Without developing my confidence and courage on the back of that little black pony, I cannot say for certain that I would be where I am today.

I have learned to trust my intentions, efforts, and abilities even when they have been tested, even when I have done things that require self-reflection and forgiveness. I trust people even after I have gone through situations where I question whether I ever should. It was never about perfection with Smokey. It was about the journey of getting it done. When I think back on my rides with him, I am reminded that the lesson is in the journey and to learn something valuable will beat the pursuit of perfection every single time.

Creating and growing a business is all about progress over perfection. Any progress takes confidence and courage to keep moving forward. In 2017 I committed to showing up for myself and the equestrian community by creating a business that helped other equestrian women. I wasn't exactly sure what having "an impact" looked like, but that was something that I desired.

When I was packing up my classroom on my last June as a classroom teacher, I was told that "people" were saying I was leaving teaching because I had a mental breakdown. I found this interesting for two reasons. Firstly, none of the people who cared to speak *about* me cared enough to speak *to* me. This told me that it was not being said by the ones who mattered most to me, so it did not matter. And secondly, I felt like I was leaving for the exact opposite reason, but often brave and confident action is seen as crazy and irrational by outsiders looking in.

In the last four years, Nikki Porter Coaching has shifted and transformed just as much I did personally leading up to launching my business. Every day it feels more my own, which is funny because it is the most "my own" thing I have ever had. It has my ideas, my lessons, my answers, my desires, my hopes, and my dreams for myself and equestrian women everywhere, all wrapped up in one. Creating and growing the business has been the ultimate test for *every* lesson my horses have taught me, but maybe it has tested me in a lesson I learned from Valhalla more than any other I have been taught.

I was reminded recently that horsemanship is all about opposites. My transitions from one horse to the next seemed to follow that theory nicely. I had outgrown Little Smokey, and it was time to move up. As a result of this move, I found myself on the back of yet another gray mare with a strong sense of self-preservation; only this time, I was ready for a new lesson.

I swear my next pony began teaching me what I needed most from the second I saw her. I was walking next to my grandfather toward the show barn at the exhibition grounds, and I saw someone I did not know holding a pony I had never seen before. We were on the hunt for my next partner, but I'm not even sure I knew what I was looking for until I saw her that day.

As we approached her, I whispered to my papa, "I want her." The funny thing is, I could see in the way he looked at me that he wanted me to have her too. I honestly don't remember how the rest took place; all I remember is being told we were taking her home for a trial, and I knew that meant she was going to be mine.

I soon discovered that "Hally" was one of the special ones, according to my papa, as he educated me on what two tight forehead swirls meant about a horse's personality. Much like my first pony, it was as if my papa and my pony were working together to teach me what I needed to learn the most.

Soon after purchasing Hally, I was told a disturbing story about her and learned exactly why purchasing her was easier for my parents than I had anticipated. I was informed that a Canadian Olympic rider had visited our area that spring, and a well-known local rider took the clinic on Hally. In the span of an hour lesson, the rider fell off multiple times, and with the ear of my pony tight in her grip, the clinician told the owners she should be shot. I didn't understand why anyone would say that about this incredible pony until I realized it was because they weren't willing to listen to her.

It became known through trial and error that we had to make our ideas seem like Hally's ideas for us to work well together. She slowed me down, she made me think, and she forced me to *listen* like no other. We saw a lot of struggle and success in the short two years I owned her. I felt more connected to her than I ever knew possible to connect to another being. I could feel her thoughts and her emotions, and she could feel mine. Luckily, we were both set on understanding each other, and when we both learned to listen, we felt unstoppable.

Listen. Just stop talking and listen. I repeated those words in my head over and over while surrounded by the palm trees and the hot magical air of Costa Rica. In November of 2018, I attended a personal development and spiritual retreat on a mission to come home ready to create some momentum in my business and life. I did a lot of listening that week: to my mentors, to the ocean, to friends, and to myself. I listened when I needed to move. I listened when I needed to eat. I listened when I needed to speak. I listened when I needed silence and when I needed to be silent.

During one writing exercise we were prompted to do mid-week, I got quiet. I heard, loud and clear from deep in my soul, that I needed to forgive. Without really thinking, I frantically wrote a letter to both myself and to the family member who had silenced me. They denied me of not only feeling and expressing but denied me a relationship I desperately thought I wanted and needed in my life.

Holding onto the hurt, resentment, and pain was keeping me quiet, small, and out of reach to become who I was setting out to be. Due to my lack of forgiveness, I was still sitting quietly, sipping tea through gritted teeth; the good girl, managing the ease of others, the girl that I used to be.

I burned that letter. I learned that all relationships that end must do so for the world to make sense to the person who ends them, but this was important for my own growth as well. That day, I made a commitment to myself to live openly and honestly in a way that terrified and excited me at the same time.

When I returned home from that trip, I hit send on my first manuscript. I held my first published book, *The Conscious Communicator*, in my hands on the last day of 2018. In November of 2019, I launched my first podcast, *Take the Reins: A Personal Growth Podcast for Horse Owners*. In October of 2020, I launched *Informed Equestrian* with my friend and business partner, Nadine Smith, leading into my second podcast, Canada Horse Podcast.

In January 2021, I created my first group coaching program with my mentor and friend, Beth Anstandig, of the *Circle Up Experience*. In August of that same year, I led sixteen incredible women on the journey of sharing their stories of tests and transformations through horses in this very book.

Not only have I got up from the table, but I have also found my voice and am committed to using it to help others find theirs. The stories you have read, the tests you have witnessed through their words, and the transformations of these equestrian women you walked alongside are just the beginning for us all. We have been tested and transformed, but we are far from done, and we are proud to speak up and be the women we were born to be.

About Nikki Porter

———

Nikki is an Equestrian Mindset Coach, author, and podcast host. She teaches personal growth specifically designed for equestrians which is informed for and by the horses we love so deeply. Her work enhances the mindset to shift her clients from feeling disconnected, frustrated, and anxious to being connected, present, and confident in and out of the tack. Her teaching translates seamlessly into an equestrian's work with their equine partners, allowing them to become the horse owner they long to be while navigating their personal growth journey.

Nikki lives in Amherst, Nova Scotia with her husband Mike and their daughter Blake, dog Paris, and her horse, Ford.

Dedication

To Mike, my husband, who encourages me to be the best rider and person I can be.

BOOK RECOMMENDATIONS

Cleaning Up Your Mental Mess by Dr. Caroline Leaf
Braving the Wilderness by Brené Brown
Greenlights by Matthew McConaughey

OTHER PUBLICATIONS BY NIKKI PORTER

The Conscious Communicator: The Pursuit of Joy and Human Connection Inspired by the Art of Horsemanship
Let's Be Honest: Your Equestrian Journey Starts with You
Let's Ride: Taking the Reins on your Equestrian Goals
Let's Get to Work: Bridging the gap between self-discovery & horsemanship (available soon)
We Are Unbreakable: Raw, Real Stories of Resilience (co-author)
Take the Reins Podcast: A Personal Growth Podcast for Horse Owners
Canada Horse Podcast (co-creator/host)

Manufactured by Amazon.ca
Bolton, ON

23868262R00120